LIVING ON LAUGHTER

A Memoir of a Former Humor Columnist and Newspaper Publisher

Anne Spry

Flint Hills Publishing

Cover Design by Amy Albright

Author Photograph by Timeless Portraits

(Flint Hills Publishing

Topeka, Kansas
Tucson, Arizona
www.flinthillspublishing.com

Printed in the U.S.A.

Paperback Book: ISBN: 978-1-966323-36-5
Electronic Book ISBN: 978-1-966323-37-2

Library of Congress Control Number: 2025916888

Dedication

To all the former readers of Letters from Home in *The Caldwell County News*

A Note from the Author

Introducing Some Universal Characters and Life Experiences

You are about to meet a few individuals who bear some odd names—Mad Mother, The Kid, Big Guy, Lemonade Man, and Motorcycle Mama. These were the names I gave myself, my son, my second husband, and my mother while writing a humor column for *The Caldwell County News* from the 1980s until I sold the newspaper in 2013. The intent at the time of the column writing was to give my readers a way to put themselves into the stories that depicted what I hoped were universal life experiences. These were stories about raising a child, watching the strange antics of a city-guy-turned-small-town/country man, and the stupid predicaments I got myself into during my few years as a divorced mother trying to do home repair and maintenance. And run a newspaper in a tough economy without running it into the ground. Add to these stories some tales about aging, and we may have a recipe for lots of things to laugh about.

The book you are reading was first published as a collection of humor and philosophical columns in 2014, the year I got my start at a retirement career of book publishing. The decision to republish and refurbish *Letters from Home: Adventures with Mad Mother, Lemonade Man and The Kid* by Anne Tezon occurred shortly after Flint Hills Publishing completed another memoir of mine, *Taking the Long Way Home: A Peace Corps Memoir of Brazil.* The republishing was prompted partly by changes in my own life circumstances as well as changes in reader habits. Publisher Thea Rademacher almost choked when I told her the original book contained almost 300 pages and a whopping 497,000 words. Sheesh! I embarrassed myself with all those words that not too many people read. And there were mistakes in the first book in addition to all the extra words since I edited and proofread it myself.

Lemonade Man died in 2015. I started a new book publishing and memoir business in 2016. I sold our house in Kansas City and moved back to my first home in Kansas. I remarried in 2018. My last name is now Spry. All this, plus creeping into the so-called golden years, has made me intent on solidifying my legacy as a writer.

Re-reading these columns has brought me lots of laughter as I relived my life. The laughter brought out the endorphins that have been lurking in my brain under a cloak of seriousness and a commitment to service and volunteerism that have plagued my retirement life. May reading *Living on Laughter* bring out all your endorphins, as well, or at least a chuckle or two.

Part 1:

Laughing at the Kid Until He Becomes a Big Guy

A little backstory…

My son Michael was born January 2, 1984. After taking two rounds of fertility pills, suffering a miscarriage on the weekend I took over The Hamilton Advocate-Hamiltonian from a third-generation owner, I had almost despaired of having children. I was 34, so he was cherished from the first moment I held him in my arms. I recall writing his birth announcement and a column while still incarcerated with him at Research Hospital. The poor kid didn't have a clue for several years that he would be the subject of many subsequent Letters from Home, *as my personal columns were called. As he grew, he came to the newspaper office frequently. I have a photo of him with a bottle hanging out of his mouth while playing on my computer (or it may have been a typewriter back then) with editor Dennis Cox standing behind us.*

The newspaper was one big family back then, with the employees forming a tight-knit group. Meeting weekly deadlines and staying at the office sometimes through the wee hours when we faced equipment malfunctions and breakdowns made us closer (after we were able to get some sleep and get over the "grumpies" induced by stress).

Michael began working at the newspaper office as a youngster, stuffing inserts in the paper and sometimes going with me to make deliveries of shoppers and a real estate/lifestyle guide. He even wrote some sports stories. When he became a high school student, his friends and classmates began teasing him whenever he was the subject of a column. That's when I changed his column moniker from The Kid *to* Big Guy.

Through a divorce from his dad in 1990, and adjusting to a new stepdad in 1995, Michael was a good sport about his appearances in Letters from Home. *The original* Letters from Home *book was primarily intended as the story of his young life. I sure hope he doesn't mind this reprise. I certainly enjoyed it and laughed out loud a few times.*

Travels with baby, a/k/a breaking the law

This week's chapter of the baby care book is entitled "Travels with Baby." The Kid took his first lengthy car trip last weekend. The three of us are not too much worse for the wear, but there are some definite logistical problems in traveling with a three-month-old.

The first problem is the famous infant seat. You know, the one that it's illegal to travel without? If you've never been riding in a compact car with a child in a plastic contraption in the back seat arching his back and screaming, you just haven't lived. Another interesting feat with the infant seat is feeding. Breast feeding. Impossible to do it in the car without breaking the law.

So, we decide to keep the infant seat and the infant separated for the feeding. While preparing to burp, we were caught off guard by his father hissing, "Get him down! There's a patrolman!" While I was hiding my fugitive son until we passed by the friendly radar man, a/k/a infant seat enforcer, I got a lap full of spit up.

After our first experience in travels with baby, I can tell you that a lap full of baby puke is preferable to what you get when you change dirty pants at 55 mph. *March 1984*

Observing the two-footed, poop-tailed gooney bird

This week we take a trip to the remotest regions of Northwest Missouri to observe wildlife in its natural setting. We're watching the two-footed, poop-tailed gooney bird. The creature we have spotted today is male and happens to be about ten months old. We're most concerned with recording the feeding habits of this gooney bird, including:

•Never sitting down to eat and never presenting his mouth anywhere near the proffered food.

•Escaping like a miniature Houdini from any strap placed by the adults in the feeding chair. The ten-month-old gooney is especially adept at sliding and wriggling out of any restraints, then smiling at himself with satisfaction and babbling with pleasure. This is often followed by a bobbing dance and repeated attempts to jump out of the feeding chair.

• If any morsels being fed to the gooney should fall out of the spoon and onto the tray of the chair, the creature immediately pounces on it and smears it all over.

•If the gooney could talk, he would tell the adults that he prefers to eat standing at his mother's side and getting his dirty hands all over her clothing. Furthermore, he would announce that he clearly prefers to ingest potting soil and toilet paper to anything put out by gooney food manufacturers. In the absence of such tasty fare, he'd just as soon eat crumbs off the floor left over from the previous meal.

•If any of the gooney's food does stay in his mouth, his favorite game is to "do the raspberry," especially when forced to eat apple-blueberry gooney food. Try getting *those* stains out in the laundry.

Maybe on the next safari we can take a more detailed look at the growth and progress of these fascinating creatures in Northwest Missouri's wild kingdom. *October 1984*

When is now over so later can start?

It's about time Mom let me take over her column. I was about to demand equal time when she got lazy and let me have at the computer. It's my turn to give a kid's point of view about all these complaints you've been hearing.

In the first place, parents are pretty dumb. And they don't know how smart we are. As an active 15-month-old, I've been learning the greatest tricks. Tricks like climbing. I climb up on the couch and dive head-first into the playpen, and for some strange reason, my mom is always sucking in her breath. She's going to give herself a chronic case of the hiccups.

She and Dad think it's pretty neat when I learn these tricks. They just don't want me to know that. Like the time I climbed up on the stool and then into the bathroom sink and ate soap. They thought it was so neat they took my picture. But then they made me get down and haven't let me get up there again.

That sink stopper is one of the best toys to put in your mouth. But Mom about throws up when she catches me doing that. She says,

"People spit in that sink, you little idiot!" I wonder if I could call the hotline for verbal child abuse.

They laughed a lot at me the day I learned to take my jacket and push it at them to let them know I wanted outside. But do you think that works? They just laugh or try to ignore me and say, "Not now." I'd like to know when "now" is over and "later" starts.

The few times they do let me out of prison, I go bananas. There's so much to look at—birds, dogs, cars, and trees. And there's lots on the ground to taste. But all of a sudden, Mom is saying bad things about what she'll do to the next dog she catches in our yard.

The thing I like the most about outside is this great, hard place that you can run on. But Mom says I need to learn just what "street" means and that it's off limits to little kids. But I think she's probably going to have to build a fence in our yard to keep me away from it. Then I'll have a new trick to learn in seeing if I can climb over or under that! *March 1985*

The imitation is better than the real thing

Whoever said that imitation is the sincerest form of flattery must have had a child tagging along behind them.

It can bring a parent up short to realize that she has a little shadow who suddenly takes great pains to put his hands on the side of the bathtub exactly as she does when drawing water for the nightly chore. Or to see him thinking hard and trying to fold his arms across his chest and look disgusted like his mother does when he makes her mad.

The classic example of the shadow syndrome is putting on Mom or Dad's shoes. Our photo album contains one snapshot of a child who is all boots. We never got to photograph the extreme irritation that resulted when he walked out of them and couldn't get them back on.

If you want to be scientific instead of poetic, you can say that imitating parents is one way of learning to function in the human world. The animal too, I guess.

The animal comes out in our shadow when he imitates us

scolding. A, "Don't hit!" from one of us prompts an immediate, "Don't hit! Right now! I mean it!"

The first few times were funny and cute. Not so much now. And it's gone beyond the imitation stage. Now when he puts on my shoes, it's not to imitate me. It's to keep me from leaving for work. *May 1986*

If you can't ride it, it's broken

The growing reasoning powers of a two-year-old are fun to watch. Often, I find myself wishing I could get by with some of the reactions to problems our son has.

Upon being introduced to a tricycle that was a little tall for his legs, The Kid insisted it was broken. He couldn't ride it, so it had to be broken.

Of course, any book that he hasn't committed to memory is "broken" too. He takes after his paternal grandfather, walking around mumbling bits of verse or nursery rhymes that he's memorized. But when his grandfather fails to remember a line, he slides right over it. Not The Kid. He gives an exasperated sigh and says, "Mommy, can't read it!" even though the book he's quoting from isn't in front of him.

The other day at the supper table he was begging for more "lettuce with clothes on it." He looked at our quizzical expressions as if to say, "Dressing, you dummies." *May 1986*

Life is full of conditionals, kid

The mind of a two-year-old has trouble grasping some of the finer subtleties of life. The Mad Mother's kid sees no gray areas—only wants and dislikes. And he demands instant gratification or relief from discomfort.

He has yet to learn the following:

•You have to eat your beets in order to get any dessert.

•You have take off your shoes before jumping into a swimming pool or bathtub.

•You have to take a nap before getting a treat.

•You have to smile and act cute and give Mom a kiss if you want something. (He's catching on to this one.)

•It's a requirement of life to pick up your toys before going outside.

•Saying things like, "All done," and, "That's all folks" does not necessarily mean the end of church services. It sometimes works for bath time and old cartoons.

If the Mad Mother was a little *smarter,* she might be able to put a name to the thought processes that occur when a child finally grasps the fact that certain behavior produces certain results, and that life is full of many conditionals. Right now, it's all she can do to cope with potty training. *June 1986*

A two-year-old visits the twilight zone regularly

There is a murky twilight zone in the brain of a two-year-old—before it gets set in the mold of obstinate three-year-old—where language isn't processed well and where the senses are confused.

The Mad Mother's son has been showing signs of such confusion lately when he tells me he smells his grandfather coming, or he smells a tractor on the road. And he sees a policeman's siren with his ears. Poor kid.

He's not sure about the function of a stomach. One night he woke up crying from too many garden cucumbers. I gave him a Tums and told him it would make his tummy feel better, whereupon he lifted up his t-shirt, laid the Tums on his stomach, and went back to sleep.

The other day he was eating a sandwich and wanted to know where mine went. I informed him that I'd already eaten mine and that it was in my stomach. He promptly stuffed his peanut butter and jelly sandwich down his shirt and patted his stomach to indicate that's where his was too.

His confused state is further evident these days in his plaintive question every half hour or so—"Mom, what am I doing?"

We may have a kindergarten flunkout on our hands. Or a nosy

news reporter. *July 1986*

The gentle art of food mutilation

If mutilating food was a crime, our son would have been locked up long ago.

We watch in fascination like zookeepers as our own monkey makes snakes and "wormies" out of bread, strains cottage cheese through his fingers, and puts the crush on a tomato slice. Liberal child raisers would tell us that he's being creative and has to feel the textures of food and manipulate them to see how they react.

There's not going to be too much protest from a tomato as it gets squished, but there's plenty of protest from a two-year-old when his plate is whisked away because he hasn't given it the respect food deserves. Crocodile tears fall from his eyes as a glass of water is thrown down the drain because he's gone fishing in it.

We wonder sadly why mealtime has to be a proving ground for authority and why food becomes an "airplane" so it doesn't have to come anywhere near The Kid's mouth.

The end of mealtime at our house is like a Chinese fire drill. You get up quickly and move out of range of some of the grimiest hands in the world, hands that don't seem to want to conform to the mold of a spoon handle because the brain it's connected to is too lazy to command it. Besides, it's faster to scoop up Jell-0 and cottage cheese in a fist and a daring challenge to eat catsup with two fingers.

The stage between potty training and animal eating behavior and behavior that doesn't require regular hosing off has to be one of the more frustrating times for parent zookeepers. *August 20, 1986*

From imaginary playmates to make-believe parents

Our resident child prodigy scolds someone all the time. The other day, while in the bathtub, he started talking to his "other mother." He said she was under the water in the tub. He explained he had a big mommy and a little mommy. I didn't dare ask him which one I was.

The other Mommy is the one that never yells at him and gives him all the popsicles and soda pop he wants. He can probably stuff her in a closet when he doesn't want her to see things she doesn't approve of. What a deal!

I might feel bad about this imaginary parent if The Kid didn't talk to flies and bugs too. His conversation with the flies usually occurs after a meal when he wants to go outside, and I don't want him to. He ends up holding the door open interminably, and when I holler, "Shut the door, you're letting in the flies," he strikes up a conversation. Most of it is authoritative, with him telling the dumb critters to "get out of here." But these are no ordinary flies. Nope. They're all French flies. *September 1986*

Mommy's little tomato burner

About every other day, the Mad Mother becomes firmly convinced that she's too old to have a two-year-old. When he insists on washing his Stomper car in his glass of milk or says that his milk itself needs washing off with a washcloth, somehow the energy to explain why these actions are not acceptable just ebbs away. She finds herself staring, glassy-eyed, and just letting him get away with anything, simply too tired to protest.

But occasionally there is a glimmer of hope. You see that someday he might grow up to be a help to you in your old age. Just the other day, the Mad Mother had some unexpected help while peeling tomatoes for canning.

It was a case of not having the energy to explain why a two-year-old shouldn't be helping can tomatoes. Much to the Mad Mother's surprise, he put the tomatoes in the colander, moved his chair over to the stove, plopped the things in the boiling water, one-by-one, watched them for a few seconds, then fished them out with a scoop and brought them back over to her. Amazing! He had quite a system worked out. When his aunt walked in, open mouthed at the scene and his adeptness, he calmly informed her that he was "burning the tomatoes."

He can burn all the tomatoes he wants if he does it that well.

Mad Mother recalls being that enamored of doing dishes when she was his age. That novelty lasted about a year at most.

If only he'd take as much interest in picking up toys as he does in burning tomatoes. *September 17, 1986*

Why, oh why do they whine?

A mother cannot imagine anything more irritating in the world than to be fixing dinner and having a kid hanging on her, whining incessantly. You try to be understanding, blaming hunger pangs. But the understanding wears off when they whine through the meal and don't eat, even when you play "airplane" with the food. At times like this, the "hangers" just won't open to let anything in.

Well, the Mad Mother decided recently to try an experiment. Seeing that yelling and swatting the world's biggest whiner didn't get her anywhere, she recalled an episode of that quality television show, "Saturday Night Live," which featured a family of whiners.

So, the next time The Kid whined, the Mad Mother whined right back. And kept whining. At first, the reaction was a stunned silence, then a giggle. But whatever was at the root of his whining won out. It didn't work in the long run.

It did teach the Mad Mother a lesson. Whining is fun. It releases all kinds of tension. Quite satisfying, really. The next time someone comes into the office to complain about a name being misspelled or something being left out of the paper, they may get quite a surprise. Whining gets results. Maybe not the ones you ask for, but results, nevertheless. Maybe I could start whining for all our advertising. Businesses might give me more ads just to shut me up! *September 1986*

Word games to play with your toddlers

How about a game for Christmas? Want something more mind-boggling than *Trivial Pursuit* and ten times more challenging than *Wheel of Fortune*?

Try defining things for an almost-three-year-old. You can start with "good taste."

After more than two years of bending over and stretching hamstrings to shove socks on little feet and making errant arms go in small backwards holes, one morning the tyke wakes up and decides to dress himself.

Parental aggravation quickly sets in when it suddenly becomes the entertainment of the day to change socks five times and put the previous pairs into the dirty clothes hamper.

Semantics games come in when you try to explain about shirts having tails and going on tail-first instead of head-first. Also, the definition of "good taste" must be given when you come home from work and find your child wearing a gray sweat suit, yellow socks, and penny loafers. Then try your best to explain why he can't wear those things together, at least not in public.

I am not a good player at this game. In fact, I'm reduced to a state of tongue tied-ness (is that a word?) in trying to instill the concept of fear—the healthy kind—that will prevent a child from opening a car door as you're going down the road at 35 mph.

When that happened the other day, the Mad Mother was reduced to a blubbering fool. First came the shout. That was followed by stopping the car and resorting to a spanking, then an attempt to explain what could happen if he fell out and got run over.

How do you explain what death would be like? "You wouldn't be here anymore!" That's all I could come up with, besides telling him he would make his mom and dad very, very, very sad.

Our little word game has probably given him a psychosis for the rest of his life and still left him in the dark about what might happen if he plays with the lock on the car door again. I wonder if three-year-olds could be taught to play *Trivial Pursuit*? It might be easier on parents than Definitions. *December 1986*

My mom, the Christmas tree killer

If The Kid were in school (which he tells me each week he should be) he'd be writing a paper entitled, "My Mother, the Christmas Tree Killer."

I cannot tell a lie. I hustled that thing out the door while he was at his grandmother's house. I had tried to do it the day before and get him to help me. But I was told in no uncertain terms, "Don't take down Christmas, Mama. I like Christmas and I like Santa Claus!" When my back was turned, he tried to put back the wreaths that had hung on the doors.

Two days later, in his absence, I did the dirty deed, leaving evidence of the crime on the patio. It didn't take The Kid long to discover what was missing from the middle of the room.

"Where's my Christmas tree?" he demanded.

I refused to put it back.

Yes, it's been a guilt-ridden week at our house. Besides the tree episode, we had a little unpleasantness when I tried to take him home from his aunt's house. On our way out he tried to retrieve a coloring book and crayons that I was sure belonged to his cousin. He started yelling something unintelligible and looking at me with accusing eyes. He yelled all the way home, in between tears, and I was dumbfounded at the intensity of his anger. Two days later I discover that a former babysitter had brought it by his aunt's house and given it to him. Now I know what it feels like to be the perpetrator of a gross injustice.

The Kid is really getting into this righteous indignation thing. He turns it on every time I leave for work. And he's not beyond reminding us of our meal lapses. The other evening at the supper table he eyed us with disdain as we prepared to shovel in our supper. "We have to pray," he informed us.

It leaves us wondering who's running this family. But we know the answer to that question, don't we? *January 1987*

Taking advantage while Mom's on the phone

Even at the tender age of three, a youngster knows when he can make the most of a situation. Instinctively he knows when there's company in the house or when Mom is on the phone.

While long phone cords are the helpmate of a mother who's trying to get dinner or do dishes and talk to a friend, it's too much of a temptation for a little one. Our ten-foot cord has been stretched from the kitchen to the living room, used to suspend toys and wrapped around a little body five times. Suddenly you find yourself carrying on a three-way conversation with The Kid saying, "Let me talk her, Mom." He knows you don't have a hand available for spanking and that you won't anyway, until you hang up. He also knows exactly the limits of that phone cord and when to travel there when Mom has reached the limits of her patience. Murderous glances in his direction, finger-snapping, and silently mouthing threats seem to have no effect whatsoever as you hear him say, "You're funny, Mommy!"

Even worse than the distraction of a phone call at our house is Mom playing the piano. I sneaked in a few moments while I thought he was practicing his newly-acquired potty training skills. As I became re-acquainted with Chopin, my son was dumping a bottle of antibiotic from the refrigerator (when had he gotten into that?!) onto the bathroom rug, taking a tablespoon of it, and then dancing in it. All it took was about two minutes, max!

After a seat warming, tears, and a long talk about not taking medicine without Mom or Dad to help, he got what he wanted all the time—attention.

The piano lid is once again closed and the telephone cord wrapped around the top of the phone. And now that I'm ready to give him my undivided attention, he's ready to play with his trucks.

"You go work, Mom," he advises.

Thanks a lot, kid. *February 1987*

Parenthood causes strange dreams, erratic behavior

Tornado season is fast approaching. My dreams told me so. Last night's sleep had me trying to urge my family to go to the basement to escape this huge black twister bearing down on us, but nobody wanted to go down into our dirty, musty basement. We needn't have worried though, because just as it was about to strike us, it started snowing and it froze the tornado. That caused me to get mad at myself for not coming to the office to get the camera to take a photo of a frozen tornado.

It might help to know that this dream occurred after getting up at 4:30 a.m. to take a three-year-old out of Mom and Dad's bed and put him into his own.

Parenthood can be blamed for lots of erratic behavior, but sometimes the parent is not the guilty party. Just today I wondered what would have possessed me to put a bottle of Vicks in the silverware drawer. Upon taking it out to put in its proper place in the medicine cabinet, The Kid puts it promptly back in the drawer, saying that's where it belongs. If only he was that conscientious about his toys and clothes.

Erratic behavior on the part of parents can also be seen in leisure activities. On a rainy Saturday, I remembered that wonderful toy, Lincoln Logs. I made a special trip to the store just to buy a set. While there, we also bought some bubbles, another Dr. Seuss book, and then got suckered at the checkout counter into a package of gum. All that was after getting a Happy Meal at the golden arches just to get a toy robot.

As you can plainly see, parenthood makes a grown person lose their marbles. But boy, was it fun playing with Lincoln Logs again. *March 1987*

A prospect for Art Linkletter

If Art Linkletter's Show, *Kids Say the Darndest Things* was still on, the Mad Mother would try to get a ticket for her son to appear. Him and about every three or four-year-old she's come into contact with lately. Their little brain wheels churn so furiously, but you never know what will come out of their mouths, with all that thinking.

Last week The Kid went blackberry picking and for a boat ride on a local pond. Upon returning, he had to tell Mom about the trot line he'd seen. He described it as a bottle with a big fish on the end of it. When asked if it was a catfish, he replied seriously, "Yeah, it was a Garfield catfish."

A few weeks ago, we took him swimming, and upon leaving the beach area, asked him to wait for us to put on his flip-flops. To our shock, he stood still for about five minutes while we retrieved them, but he appeared deep in thought. While he was being "shoed" he started a sing-song rhyme of his own invention:

Two little flip-flops sittin' on the ground,
I'm gonna put 'em on and drown, drown, drown.

We may have to wean him from Dr. Seuss one of these days. *July 1987*

Name your ideal pet

Yesterday The Kid showed me his new friend—a box elder bug.

He was keeping it in an ashtray, complete with a few ashes, and letting it crawl all over his hands. He talked to it and even offered to let me play with it. I know Fearless Father put him up to that. He's told me many times that I've transmitted my fear of thunder and lightning to our son and was undoubtedly hoping I'd be brave and swallow my dislike of crawling things to show my approval of this new pet. I just couldn't do it.

At times like this, I'd give anything to have a house in the country. A boy needs a dog. But dogs in town just don't work. If they don't get run over, they're digging in the neighbor's trash and leaving their evidence in someone's yard to be stepped in. In the house, they shed. On a leash, they howl.

We've already considered all the options—hamsters (Mom would get to clean the cage); fish (Dad already has three that he forgets to feed, and the tank has needed cleaning for months); cats (Fearless Father ran over the last one we had); a bird (we can't stand to see something that can fly caged up).

Maybe a box elder bug isn't such a bad pet after all. They're plentiful and will last until it snows. Does anybody know what you feed a box elder bug? *November 1988*

The tooth fairy makes an appearance

The tooth fairy paid a visit to our house last week. He (she/it) came a little prematurely. Teeth aren't supposed to fall out before a kid's fifth birthday, but this one had a little help from a knee being rammed into it.

For more than a week, we cast worried glances at the mouth of The Kid, seeing one of his incisors dangling about half an inch below its twin. We watched him tear off bites of food from the sides of his mouth instead of the front. Until one day during the holidays, while playing with cousins in a big cardboard box (all those toys for Christmas and they play with a box) he hit the decisive blow. An aunt flicked it out of its hole with a finger.

They tried to prepare me for his gaping smile, but it didn't work. How vain parents are about their children's looks! Right now, with his cowlick and an inch or two more of growth, he'd be a dead ringer for Alfalfa or Spanky and *Our Gang*.

What do you suppose families, say in Africa, do when their children lose their first teeth? Do they have a "tooth fairy" rite of passage? We Americans do tend to sugar-coat certain childhood traumas. With those questions in mind, we explained the tooth fairy to a sleepy kid the night after the big loss. His only comment, as he trudged upstairs to bed, clutching his baby tooth in a paper towel, was, "But we don't have fairies in this land!"

The resident tooth fairy did her work at 6 a.m. the next day, thanking her lucky stars The Kid is a heavy sleeper. He had cousin company and didn't even think about the tooth under his pillow until someone reminded him after breakfast. He ran upstairs and, in a few minutes, we heard the excited exclamation, "I'm rich! I'm rich! My tooth turned into two quarters!" He didn't waste any time in turning those quarters into bubble gum.

Now The Kid is having a ball with the new sensation of squishing things through a hole where a tooth once lived. *January 1989*

Cooperating to build snow people

Watching four children build a snowman is like witnessing the interactions of employees of a government agency.

The Kid and his two female cousins and a male playmate took on the task of constructing their own "Frosty" in Monday's wet, heavy snow. They were promised adult assistance at the crucial moment.

The one with the loudest mouth (The Kid) was the apparent organizer and enforcer. He put his shoulder to the snow and rolled up the balls, all the while shouting orders at the other three. He paid no heed to the environmental havoc he was wreaking (taking up drought strained grass and topsoil) in his dogged pursuit of the task.

Before long, he abandoned snowball forming and stood back to let others do the dirty work. Frosty's middle section had to be put in place, a job he left for the other male, whom we'll call Playmate L. The poor kid tried everything in his power to force the heavy ball of ice onto the bottom section. At one point he had the torso up to his chest but couldn't get his knees off the ground to lift it on the top. He looked around in despair and suddenly it occurred to him that there are tools to help you do a job more easily. A nearby stick made a handy pry bar, except that snow doesn't pry.

Meanwhile, the straw boss had the head in his hands and was shouting instructions. The two girls, Cousin K and Cousin A, were standing ready to decorate the thing. No one wanted to get in the trenches and help Playmate L do the dirty work. Finally, The Kid was convinced to abandon the head for a few minutes, and the girls were enlisted to help lift the midsection. They discovered that a little cooperation goes a long way, except when the bottom ball is too pointed.

Always practical, Cousin K started kicking off the point. By that time, everybody had abandoned the scene, and it was up to faithful Playmate L to put the torso on again.

Finally, Frosty was an accomplished feat. The Kid got to put the crowning glory on and hog the credit, the girls cleaned up the mess and made it beautiful and Playmate L decided it was time to give the whole thing a big karate kick. He was stopped in mid-kick by the adult who had promised help in the beginning and had been inside watching the whole process from a window with two other mothers. This peanut gallery had been reduced to ineffectual comments and laughing at the pathetic attempts they witnessed.

Cousin A finally got around to the Equal Opportunity question. She wanted to know why you only built snow*men*.

That's when true compromise, diplomacy, and cooperation came into play. All four kids and an adult supervisor built three more snow people, a balance of male and female. These four dirty critters guard the front and back entrances to our house now, a symbol of ingenuity, cooperation, and accomplishment. Sometimes government agencies get the job done. *February 1989*

The sponge kids—alias conservation cops

Children are sponges, soaking up more than their parents realize. Only when you squeeze them do you realize what they've been learning. Sometimes the sponge is so full, things ooze out of them unsolicited. It's those things a parent should write down before they forget them in the rush of the growing up years. (This philosophical note from a woman who hasn't even filled out the baby book of her only child, who is now five).

The water shortage in Hamilton has the youngsters in The Kid's circle of friends and cousins really worried. They've been discussing it a lot lately, in between climbing the propane tank for impromptu concerts with air guitars and playing in the dust left by the drought (mud now, after last night's soaker).

These children are talking of moving to another town where there is a more ample supply of water. They're sure that's our only choice. After admonishing a kid to turn off the tap and not play in the shower, it finally hit home that water is precious and not to be wasted.

The Kid helped me plant some roses this weekend and each time I sent him to the hydrant to fill up the watering can, he came back with about two inches of water—not nearly enough to moisten the roots and give the plants a healthy start. "The reservoir is all gone," he informed me plaintively.

He also knows that the swimming pool might not open and has an alternative to propose to the city. He thinks we can fill the pool with apple juice this year. *March 1989*

A penny for your distraction

The Mad Mother is one of those people bent on eliminating wastes of time. For years, relatives by marriage (my side of the family is just like me) have made fun of me for crocheting while I watch television or for having my nose in a book while sitting at a basketball game. I can't drive the car from here to Kingston without listening to a self-improvement tape or wait to see a doctor without catching up on a professional journal.

Kansas City columnist George Gurley made fun of our type. He said we're so busy filling our lives with distractions and noise that we don't let ourselves be distracted by the really important things in life. He may have a point.

The biggest distraction in my life has been asking some extremely difficult questions lately. And he wants detailed answers. If you have any quick and easy solutions to the following puzzles, posed in a dinner hour one day (while I was trying to read the paper) please drop me a line.

1. Why do we have to have television?
2. Why do people have noses?
3. Why does there have to be spaghetti?
4. Why is there an earth? How did God make the earth?
5. Does God make houses? How come?
6. Why don't I have a baby sister?
7. Why do dogs have tails?
8. Why does bread have crusts?
9. What's your best food that's your favorite?
10. How come God makes eagles?
11. What does God make trees out of?
12. How come you need to grow up?
13. How come all the time the phone rings? *May 1989*

Will he flunk kindergarten?

I never thought it would happen to the Mad Mother.

For the past two years I've been looking forward to the day The

Kid would be ready to graduate from preschool to the real world of academics.

But last week, as I clipped the school supply list for kindergarten and put it under the refrigerator magnet, I got a bad case of butterflies. And now this week, knowing his class assignment, I can picture him in a classroom with a teacher, not just a nameless presence. Like a lot of other mothers, I'm suddenly afraid for my child to take such a big step.

The irrational thoughts that go through your mind run something like this...

• Will he get bashed on the playground when, as usual, he wants to be the boss and doesn't get his way?

• Will he drive his teacher nuts with thousands of questions?

• Will he be able to find the restroom? Will he use it once he finds it, or will he just make faces in the mirror and play in the sink?

• Will he keep his mouth shut?

• Will he find school preferable to home?

• Will he suddenly want to spend all his time with new little friends and go to their houses all the time? Will he then start to wonder why we don't have Kool-Aid, candy, and lots of other goodies in our house? Will he demand a Nintendo?

• Will he flunk kindergarten if he doesn't learn to tie his shoes?

• Will he take a nap when he's outgrown them at home?

• Will he start asking to buy designer label clothes?

• Will he eat his lunch? Who's going to threaten him with dire consequences if he doesn't?

• When he learns to read, will he ask me to stop embarrassing him by using him for column material?

Such are the selfish thoughts of a mother about to send her son into the cruel world of the playground. You'd think a fairly intelligent woman would not get so irrational. BUT HE'S MY BABY!

I may get control of myself by the second week of school.

August 1989

School: It's a whole new ball game

I'm here to report we lived through the first week of kindergarten. It was memorable. Here's an abbreviated diary.

Monday: Wild horses couldn't have kept The Kid off the school bus. Just like the letter from his teacher had suggested, we let him ride that first day and I met him at the door of the school to accompany him to class. I hope it wasn't an omen that the bus broke down by our house and after his triumphant entrance into the yellow dream machine, he promptly had to get off with the other students and onto another one. Consequently, he was late that first day and his teacher thought he'd gone to another classroom. He just about did. He was too busy acting important. I watched him walk right by me through the school doors and go upstairs with a first-grade neighbor.

The Mad Mother left work at 3:45 to be home to hear the complete story of The First Day. He and his cousin were so full of excitement, their tongues couldn't keep up. But as the evening wore on and he had time to think, he announced, "Mom, I don't think I'll go back to school. It's too hard work. It makes me tired."

Tuesday: He got his name written on the board for talking without raising his hand. I was crushed until he listed five other children who suffered similar fates.

Wednesday: He got his name written on the board again. This time it was more serious. While in line for the drinking fountain, he saw other children playing at recess and thought it must be time for him to do the same. He confessed that he had to put his head down on his desk and lost out on a playtime for that offense.

Thursday: The Kid announced at breakfast that he wouldn't be getting his name written on the board the rest of the week. He likes his teacher. Another teacher friend reports he gave her a big hug and kiss. When confronted with this, The Kid gets a funny look on his face and asks how we knew. Motivated by the jealous beast within (he rarely gives me a spontaneous hug or kiss these days) I informed him that we have spies at school, ready to report to us on whatever mischief he gets into. Poor kid.

Friday: He missed the bus for the second time this week. His eyes welled up with tears and he looked at us accusingly for taking away one of the highlights of his school day. (His Dad didn't get the soft-boiled eggs done in time.) He thinks the bus driver is one of the greatest people in the world and that 20-minute trip in the big yellow bus is evidently a pretty important sign of emerging independence.

It's becoming quite clear that starting school is almost more of an adjustment for a parent than a child. And from somewhere deep in the parental subconscious comes some familiar words: "We can't do that. It's a school night." It just spills off the tongue so naturally. *September 1989*

Playgrounds: The stuff of soap operas

The Kid is perplexed these days.

He was told on the playground recently that Rachel had broken up with him. He wanted to know exactly what that meant. So did we.

What he didn't tell us was that another little girl had accosted him on the playground and given him a big kiss. We had to rely on school spies to relate that to us. When confronted with the information, he shrugged it off and said he almost got into a fight because another boy had been chanting, "Michael's got a girlfriend!"

He said it couldn't be true because Rachel had broken up with him because she loved Will. Can you follow that?

But it seems that Will told Rachel he was breaking up with her because he wanted to play the field. Rachel was crushed and came crying to the playground monitor.

Is this a playground soap opera? Just how much do these kids know? Is it time for a talk on the birds and bees?

For crying out loud, THIS IS ONLY KINDERGARTEN!

Trying not to panic, we explain to our only offspring that we're not ready for him to settle down to one girl. That every girl in his class should be a girlfriend. After all, they're girls and he should be friendly with them. (Just not too friendly.)

I don't know what I'm getting so upset about. After all, I was teased unmercifully over a kindergarten romance. His name was

Skippy, and he had red hair and freckles. They told me he was ugly and that made me fighting mad and probably even more attracted to him.

So maybe all this is not to be worried about. It's innocent and cute. We just have to keep it that way … for the next 20 years.

In the meantime, he has more important things to worry about. Like whether he's going to get the racing set he sees advertised on television. I'll take a racing set over a girlfriend any day. *October 1989*

"What If" is replacing "Why" as the word game of choice

Remember the days when your youngster drove you crazy with all the "why" questions? Well, there's a new game in town. Between the ages of three and five, it changes to "what if."

This weekend we faced such earth-shattering scenarios as, "What if we moved to China?" The Kid needed to know if the people there would be able to talk to us and if they'd be friendly. Where would we live? How would we dress? Would it be dark on the other side of the world?

A Saturday morning drive over a river with a railroad track following the route prompted the question, "What if the railroad got covered up with water? What if there were people in a train and there was water over the tracks? Would the train become a ship and float? Where would it go?"

This makes me want to dig out an old education textbook and see what that old Frenchman Piaget had to say about this stage of mental development in children. The What If game is a lot more entertaining in a car than the Why game. It demands more imagination and less concrete information. And The Kid seems less impatient when we don't know the answer to such open-ended questions.

Yesterday The Kid's *Weekly Reader* showed pictures of scientific inventions and suggested readers draw a picture of something they'd like to invent. He drew two "electrical control towers" that he claimed would prevent houses from getting "fired" by catching all the "lightling" in the world.

As a parent watching this fascinating process of dreaming and imagination, I pray that the day will never come when it gets snuffed out by a national education system that seems to value regurgitating useless facts over playing "What If." *November 1989*

For sale: one five-year-old

Saturday, Dec. 2...For Sale: one five-year-old male. Good condition except the period from Dec. 1 to 25. During this time parents and teachers cannot understand the transformation from relative normalcy to pure obstinacy.

Needs a retread every three months or 3,000 miles, whichever comes first. (Uses the playground gravel to wear-test shoes.)

All of shots but not wormed. Definitely has ants in pants. Frequently has colds and won't blow nose. Sniffs constantly instead. Doesn't hear well, especially when told to go to bed or put away toys, though hearing checks out well at doctor's office.

Reason for selling: Parents hoarse from pleading and sometimes yelling. Price: Best offer. Will negotiate or consider trading for quiet pet that doesn't argue.

Sunday, Dec. 3...For rent: one five-year-old male. Fairly incorrigible. Doesn't like going to church because it lasts too long. Always waits until it's nearly too late to go to the bathroom. Parents need a break from constant arguments and trying to instill patience and perseverance. His grandmother says it's normal for the time of year and will get worse instead of better. Low monthly rent but must return by Dec. 24.

Monday, Dec. 4...Not for sale or rent: one five-year-old male. A friend who doesn't have children eyes him enviously. Grandmother says, "Be thankful he's healthy." The conscience reacts and wonders if he's a mirror image of parents too busy to stop and read a book or listen to his ramblings. He decorates the Christmas tree, excited because he's allowed to climb a ladder, and doesn't bunch all the decorations in one spot this year. He asks that we play some Christmas carols and says his favorite one is "The First Christmas," something he learned in school. He falls asleep curled up in a ball at his dad's feet. Much better than a dog, but with a will and mind that can't be controlled. All we can hope for is to be able to guide the will and mind in the right directions without having to resort to too much force.

Nor for sale or rent: a precious child, who, like all other children, reminds us constantly of our failings as well as our strengths, and provides a chance to enjoy the gift of life. *December 1989*

Time for a heart-to-heart

A six-year-old can develop a potty mouth overnight.

After a few years of sighing with relief when The Kid apparently ignored foul language coming from the mouths of adults and movie characters, the slang beast has come home to roost.

In a casual conversation before supper last night, The Kid said in amazement at a story I was telling, "No sh--, Mom!"

I told him his old-fashioned aunt washed his cousin's mouth out for saying the same word and it could happen to him. But how do you tell a perceptive child that it's okay for adults to say things like that but not for kids? I could have told him the hypocritical truth, that people would think bad things about his parents if they heard him say words like that.

Instead, I issued him a mild warning ticket and changed the subject. After telling him that I couldn't attend his T-ball game Saturday because I was meeting some girlfriends for lunch, he looked exasperated and said, "Mom, you can't have girlfriends. You can only have a boyfriend and that's Dad."

In vain, I attempted to explain that he had boyfriends, but he wouldn't buy it. He said girlfriends and boyfriends are who you go on dates with.

"Okay, smarty pants, what's a date?" I asked.

In total self-confidence he replied, "That's when a boy and girl go outside and give each other rings. He gets one and she gets one and it's even. And then they get married."

"Are you sure about that? Where did you learn that?" I demanded.

"On television," came the reply.

"Of course, I should've known. The same place you learned that word you said earlier."

This time he changed the subject, reminding me that there are lots of cereals on the grocery store shelves that he hadn't yet tasted, like "Fruity, Yummy Mummies" or "Count Chocula."

Only six and already he knows how to obfuscate and cuss. *June 1990*

The tyranny of La-La Land

These are the times that try parents' souls. The Summer Mother and the Sunshine Father will, in this crisis, shrink from their responsibilities and the service of their family, but everyone tells us that she who stands for it now deserves the love and thanks of grandparents, teachers, and society at large.

It's time to borrow a little from Thomas Paine to discuss a parental pain—a child who daydreams through life. How does a mother or father get them out of a semi-permanent La-La Land?

La-La Land is a hypnotic state characterized by taking 20 minutes to get socks on in the morning and missing the bus as a result. When queried, he reports that the socks stuck to his shoulder. How did they get on his shoulder? He was doing an experiment. I presume it was one on static electricity.

The cereal can't be eaten quickly enough in the morning because he has to separate the marshmallows from the little oaty-o's so he can save the good parts for last. And it takes five minutes to brush teeth because the toothpaste dispenser has to be licked spotless—never mind the mouth cooties left behind to reproduce.

In the matter of homework, a recent phenomenon, every excuse in the world can be found to shirk it. For every two minutes of work, there's five minutes of staring at the ceiling.

Take a look at the eyes during these times and they're glazed over. A shrug of the shoulders and an "I don't know" are the responses to the question, "What are you thinking about?" La-La Land has a big sign at the gate: "No parents allowed."

It wouldn't be so bad if he reserved his visits to fantasy worlds to time at home. But he must have been on a mind trip when he left a $12 souvenir hat in the restroom at school, and when he got his name on the board for not getting his schoolwork done on time.

If truth be known, he can't be held too responsible for daydreaming through life. He got a double dose from his parents, who did the same things when they were his age. He'll undoubtedly outgrow it by the time he's 35. In the meantime, it looks like we'll be making repeated visits to the school's lost and found department and going back to the child-raising guides for the chapters on teaching responsibility and staying "on task."

It's finally dawning on us that being parents is not the least bit easy. But as Thomas Paine said, "What we obtain too cheap, we esteem too lightly; 'tis dearness only that gives everything its value." He must have had his own little Paine to inspire him. *September 1990*

The Halloween that almost wasn't

Has your child ever done anything that left you totally speechless with anger? Something so bad that all you could do was scream, "Oh...Oh...How could you?"

The entire town may have heard me screaming those words Saturday.

There I was, being a proper, dutiful, loving modern mother—actually making a Halloween costume for my son. You don't catch me in that act very often. So, I must have been feeling particularly pious.

As I shelled out $6.50 for a pattern and another $ (censored–I'm too ashamed to admit how much) on four different kinds and colors of material, I asked myself, "Am I possessed, or what? Is he worth this much money and effort?"

He almost proved he wasn't Saturday.

There was already two hours invested in cutting out the dern costume one night—probably an hour longer than necessary because of two helping six-year-old hands that had trouble shoving pins into fragile tissue paper. Saturday morning cartoons provided a perfect opportunity to slip upstairs and start sewing without his help. After some side seams and leg seams, the little green thing began to take shape. Satisfied at that start, I went downstairs to make sure The Kid hadn't turned into Jimmy Jet the TV Set from being tuned in too long. I informed him that a turtle was taking shape upstairs.

With a whoop of delight, he went to inspect. That only took a few minutes, and he came down with a worried look. "Mom, I tried it on, and it was too big, so I cut it."

"You what-t-t-t!"

"I cut it. I didn't mean to," he said, backing his behind into a corner.

Even though I said, "You sure as heck better not have!" he had—two big slices.

The threats were almost as dire as the screams that the whole neighborhood surely heard. "There won't be any Halloween at our house. And you can go to school in an old sheet, for all I care!" Then came the guilt-inducing comments, like, "Do you know how much time I spent on this? Do you know how much money I spent on this?" All the time I was muttering, "I don't believe this. I just don't believe it."

It's mended, very obviously. A turtleshell will probably camouflage it. Halloween will come to our house. And no longer is there a sad-eyed child cowering on his bed. It's no big deal. But it felt big, for both of us. We're going to learn something from it. I just don't know what.

One thing we always tell ourselves in such situations—it could have been worse. He could have cut his hair down to the scalp with school scissors, like one of his best friends did. *October 1990*

The difference between men and boys is the size of their lies

Someone really ought to analyze testosterone and see what connection it has to bragging. If there is a link here, it's present as early as age seven.

Witness a conversation between two males of that age:

Kid 1: Did you know that blue whales are the biggest thing in the ocean?

Kid 2: Yeah, I knew that when I was a baby.

Kid 1: We saw one jumping out of the ocean one time ... didn't we, Mom? (A mumble or a grunt will suffice here.) And did you know they're an endangered species? When I grow up, I'm gonna hunt them and protect them.

Kid 2: So am I. Hey, did you know this hat used to belong to Elvis Presley? He wore it in one of his movies and my grandpa gave it to my dad and my dad gave it to me. And we have a check for $80,000 to prove it.

Kid 1: Really! Wow! Can I wear it?

When that request was ignored, we have a brief interruption for a "rock-out" session. A Bette Middler tape is playing on the car stereo and she's singing an old Cole Porter tune, "Miss Otis Regrets." Kid 1 says, "Hey, now that's what I call jazz!"

Mom: How do you know that's jazz?

Kid: I know everything about music. Anytime you have a zaxophone, it's usually jazz.

Mom: The word is "saxophone" and you're mostly right.

Kid: Yeah, that's what I said ... zaxophone. Anyway, I live for music.

Mom: Now that's a story I believe, since you know all the lyrics to all the old songs.

Kid: Yeah, that's because I listen to Oldies 95 all the time.

On another occasion, I'd swear he's been reading all my self-improvement books about dreaming big dreams in detail.

All the way to Kansas City, he outlined his plans for a clubhouse he's planning to build. That dream involves a two-story model with "electrical fence around the top, booby traps, a telescope, binoculars for everyone, American flags, a megaphone for saying

'Who Goes There?!' and 'What's the password?' and a sign that says, "Girls Not Allowed."

The detail is further outlined in plans to call all his uncles to come over with their toolboxes in the morning. A truck will deliver the lumber and Mom will make lunch. At the last minute, he decides he might want to take down the sign disallowing girls because those females might come in handy in the construction phase, especially if it's to get done by noon so everyone can have lunch and play in it.

Now we have an idea that fish stories and tall tales have their origins in male hormones. Whoever said that the difference between men and boys is the size of their toys knew what she was talking about. She just left off the bragging part. *September 1991*

The mathematical genius of an eight year old

The child who got bored stiff with adding and subtracting in second grade but loved multiplying is now trying his hand at real money situations. He's not doing so well. And when you put his cousin into the equation, the mathematical calculations become even more convoluted.

It was J.C. Penney Days and the $2 The Kid had left over from allowance was burning a hole in his fanny pack. His cousin started the day with $11.

The first thing they spotted at the flea market was a Styrofoam glider. What a bargain! You got two for only $1! There went $1. The second dollar was frittered away on candy or gum. Then, Cousin goes into the banking business and loans The Kid $1 for another set of gliders, so he can have a whole fleet of fighter planes. Enter a friend of The Kid, who also comes in line for a loan and purchases a fancy pocketknife from one of the booths.

All of a sudden, The Kid "finds" a $5 bill. He figures "finders-keepers" and promptly buys ten more gliders. Sometime later, cousin discovers he's missing $5. By then, Kid's friend has left after surrendering the pocketknife and probably getting in big-time trouble with his mom. The two remaining math geniuses get their heads together and approach Grandma and Grandpa with a plan:

Why not take the money they're getting from selling wooden crafts at the flea market and give it to them so they can buy more gliders, or at least a carnival ride?

While giving them credit for ingenuity in the financial world, Grandma and Grandpa don't bite on that one. The boys go home with a bag full of Styrofoam gliders, four of which are now on the roof of the house and one of which ended up in the dog's mouth.

Now I know why The Kid just loves the famous children's book, *Alexander, Who Used to Be Rich Last Sunday.*

Is eight too young to open a savings account? *June 1992*

Kid does his own talking head routine for Presidential election

My in-house political advisor peeked around the corner last night after his shower and said cryptically, "Don't trust Perot!"

I looked up from the magazine I was reading and asked why.

"Because he got in the race, then he changed up his mind. You can't trust him!"

The Kid then came into the living room and added, "Besides, he has funny ears."

I started to tell him that we shouldn't vote for or against someone just because of the way they look, but decided I'd be fighting a losing battle against more people than just the one in my own house.

My political advisor then plopped on the couch and started doing aerobics (a neat trick when you're wrapped in a towel) and continued his tirade against politicians.

"You shouldn't vote for Clinton either. He said he'd give everybody a million dollars if he's elected, but then he said he wouldn't."

My raised eyebrows didn't stem that fabrication from his overactive imagination. But his next sentence led me to believe that he'd merely been picking up the general drift of this political campaign and was just trying to hold an adult conversation at the ripe age of eight.

"You can count on Bush," he said with conviction. Keep in mind that this is the same child who, only a few hours earlier, had announced, "Mom, did you know that a Super Nintendo is only $56? You can get it at Wal-Mart, where they have everyday low prices." Proof positive of the brainwashing of our children. Not only do they memorize commercials, but they also pick up subtle nuances and sound bites from news broadcasts.

"Mom, is Bush going to come to Missouri to vote for himself for president?" was the next political question of the evening.

"No dear, he'll vote where he lives. But I guess he has been in Missouri a lot lately, hasn't he? Missouri's an important state in the election."

Before he went to bed with the funny papers, my child-turned-political-savant surprised me with a question that showed he doesn't have the slightest idea what a political subdivision is. What a relief. He had me worried I might have to watch more television just to keep up with him. *October 1992*

When it comes to comparative fractions, being a parent is hard work

A fourth grader is a strange creature.

This is the age when the world of knowledge opens up and the little suckers get greedy for all they can stuff into their heads.

Thing is, it's pretty taxing for the parents.

This week we've had discussions on the meaning of infinity and a quiz on the capitals of nearly every country in the world. I now know the smallest country and the least populous one. And instead of reading a newspaper at the breakfast table, The Kid pores over a road atlas and tries to find the highest spot in Missouri, which, for some strange reason, I did already know.

Last week it was comparative fractions and the Mad Mother just about panicked. When my breathing returned to normal, I remembered in a flash of inspiration the Graduate Record Exam review book buried in the bottom of the closet. It had a math section that included a basic review of fractions.

Calmly (or a reasonable facsimile thereof) I explained to The Kid how you compare fractions, and suddenly a light bulb went on, replacing the tears that had threatened a few moments before when the process was a mystery.

Whew! Winged that one, didn't you?! I told myself with relief after my son had hugged me in gratitude for helping him with his lessons. But now I'm worried. What comes after comparative fractions? Already I've flunked fourth grade physics because I never learned the differences between radiation, convection, and that other C word —oh yeah, conduction.

This is the age when you suddenly want to buy a set of encyclopedias and the biggest dictionary ever published. The only easy question I've been asked in the past two weeks by my fourth grader is, "Mom, were you a hippie in the sixties?"

I'm wondering if the school district would consider publishing a review booklet or a Cliff's Notes on every homework subject that's likely to come up in the next eight years. It could sure be a life (face) saver. *February 1994*

The difference between male and female Lego-maniacs

There must be something to recent controversial allegations that males and females have very different brain functions. You don't even have to watch Oprah to know that men and women think differently.

Take the subject of Legos. A book I'm reading says that male children like to build tall, complex things out of blocks that they can later knock down. Girls, given the same set of blocks, build horizontal structures that are stable and domestic. Now that makes me feel less guilty about my disinterest in helping my son build Lego contraptions that only later were found in shambles on the living room floor.

Yes, The Kid is a confirmed Lego-maniac. Even at the ripe old age of ten, he hones in with his Lego radar on the latest set to be issued from a company dedicated to depriving parents of their retirement incomes. This child will spend an hour at the Lego display of any Wally World, becoming clearly agitated when I give him a hairy eyeball and a two-minute warning to get out of the toy aisle unless he wants to see an exploding mother.

This weekend he decided to get his Legos organized. Out came the flat box that a mountain of microscopic and colorful plastic has been stored in. Within an hour, without instructions, he reassembled a space buggy, a galactic something-or-other, a space shuttle, an ice sled, and a motorcycle. The buddy who joined his Legos with The Kid's is just out of luck, because these re-created things are to be permanently enshrined on new shelving promised by a mother who wants to see toys off the floor of a room that would easily qualify for disaster assistance.

Now that those tasks are completed, it's time to get out the Lego catalog conveniently included with each set sold. After remaining unconvinced that my child requires a monorail, a galactic space center, and a $75 contraption with motor and moving parts, I made the flippant remark, "Where are the Legos for girls?"

There they were, in the back of the book. All pink and green. There were sets showing beach houses and boats, boutiques and bathrooms, complete with little Lego girls and boys. Instead of space helmets and lasers, these cute little creatures were carrying barbecue spatulas and sporting sunglasses. They were driving boats through cool lagoons and relaxing under palm trees. "Now this, I could get into," I said.

"Those things don't sell very well," said The Kid, snatching the catalog away from me and returning to his dreams of future Star Wars-type battles to be fought with little plastic things under his command.

Yes, my confirmed Lego-maniac has shown me clearly the difference between the bright red and blue of boy Legos and the hot pink and green of girl Legos, between wars and beach vacations. And he reminds me there aren't too many shopping days left until Christmas. *November 1994*

Breaking a world record for Styrofoam shot put

Take the hottest week of the year. Throw two 11-year-old boys in the back seat of a car loaded to the gills. Mix well with pop and a few hundred miles of travel and you have the recipe for a vacation straight out of a Hollywood comedy. Make that a horror film

The adults on our trip would have preferred to spend the entire week sipping cold beverages, reading and chilling out by the pool. Instead, we visited Dinosaur World, hiked through a cave, rented a fishing boat, and took a steam locomotive through the Arkansas woods. We went souvenir shopping at a quaint village and "Batman Forever" viewing at a theater in Oklahoma City. By the end of all this, we were looking forward to going back to work to rest.

Too bad someone didn't tell us not to go fishing with two squirmy boys on Beaver Lake on one of the hottest days of the year. The scene we made was pure comedy as we looked for a shady spot because it was beastly hot at 8 a.m., then getting fishing lines tangled up in trees and losing bait on snags. Women with weak kidneys do not make for good fishing buddies. Neither do little boys who want to change bait and bobbers every five minutes.

By the time we went souvenir shopping in Eureka Springs, the adults separated from the boys with a promise to reunite at a designated hour. Yes, we admit it. We turned them loose on an unsuspecting group of merchants whose main attraction for 11-year-old males is plastic snakes and t-shirts advertising Bear Whiz Beer.

The highlight of the trip was the ride home. By that time, entertainment consisted of picking on each other. So, to distract the back seat, we stopped at a drive-in for two large cherry limeades—one for the front seat and one for the back. Two miles down the road, from the back seat we hear, "Um ... Mom, there's like, a little leak in this cup."

The little leak consisted of a straw rammed through the side of the cup. After a futile attempt to put my finger in the Styrofoam dike and stem the tide of red oozing out, I rolled the window down and littered for the first time in my adult life.

Five miles later, when the tires hit a bump, the large limeade on the dash of the car cascaded into my lap, spilling into my purse and streaming down my legs. In the parking lot of a closed farm supply store, I attempted to set a world's record for shot-putting Styrofoam. Meanwhile, from the back seat, one boy was bawling and screaming because the other had pinched the wart on his elbow.

Such are the golden moments of our lives—the ones we laugh about when we're old. *July 1995*

The excuses of a 13-year-old who doesn't want to shuck sweet corn

Thirteen-year-old males have a good thing going in life, speaking in gross generalizations. They think that food magically appears on the table, that their clothing gets washed by invisible hands, and appears folded in their drawers. They probably also assume that milk comes from the grocery store and that green beans grow in cans.

The Kid isn't quite that naive, especially after a weekend of helping put up a corn crop. However, he is extremely imaginative and ingenious at making up excuses not to work. He's on the cusp of the harsh world of adulthood—tall enough to make you think he's 15 or 16, but young enough to run and play, tease and torment, with the best of his peers.

We're easing him into the world of work and adult responsibilities. One day a week he stuffs inserts into the newspaper and counts out shoppers for bundling. For that he is paid a nominal fee. Of that nominal fee, he gets to pocket about 25% and puts the remainder into a savings account. His allowance works the same way. For making his bed, doing his laundry, mowing the lawn, and doing doggie poop patrol in the back yard, he earns a meager $8 a week. He keeps $3 and throws $5 into the brandy snifter on the kitchen counter. That container is his Christmas Club fund. These object lessons in savings appear to have been implemented just in the nick of time. He's already informed us he doesn't want any two-pair-for-$30 Walmart shoes for school this year.

We thought it was time he got a closer look at the process of putting food away for a rainy, cold day. The two of us headed south for Motorcycle Mama's house, where four rows of sweet corn awaited processing. He tried his darndest to get out of the trip, first with the announcement that he'd have to do the same thing at his other grandmother's house, and then with an attempt to get dumped off at a cousin's house on the way down south. Neither ploy worked and a threatened pout was forestalled by two stops at the golden arches for his favorite fuel.

Once at Grandma's, The Kid became invisible, quietly inconspicuous while we canned beets and shredded zucchini the first evening. The next morning was show time. Grandpa enlisted a younger back to help pick and shuck hundreds of ears of sweet corn, while the females sweated over boiling pots of water and squirting corn cobs.

Afternoon came, and with it another 100-degree scorcher. We didn't have quite enough corn to fill the freezer, so it was back to the corn patch, this time for me and The Kid. Suddenly, with Mom instead of Grandpa, there was some reluctance to buckle down to the job at hand. First, he tried whining, "Why do I have to do this? Don't we have enough already?" followed by, "It's too hot!"

That failing, he tried bluffing, only half teasing when he said, "I'm going to the house. I'm going right now!" I tried the old counting trick I used to employ when he was five. "You better get back here before I count to ten or else!" That sounded entirely ridiculous used on a 13-year-old. Next in the bag of tricks was THE LOOK. It worked enough to get him back to shucking. That's when his creativity kicked in.

"Look at this headbanger!" he said, showing me how a corn cob with flying silk does a good imitation of a rock star.

In desperation, I divided the remaining corn crop into two piles. "Let's see who can shuck the fastest. Ready, set, go!" It worked.

Now when he eats corn this winter, I'll remind him of the hand he had in it and he'll look at Lemonade Man, who somehow managed to wangle out of the corn trip, and say, "I recognize these kernels. They came from headbanger."

I've explained to him he was lucky that he didn't have to weed the garden AND pick and shuck the corn. He remained unconvinced. Maybe we can all have a good laugh over a big helping of corn one of these days—when he's 30. *July 1997*

This sport must be a testosterone thing

Imagine this: a bunch of women get dressed up in camo gear and go to the woods with toy guns and shoot each other with paint.

If you think something's wrong with that picture, you're not alone. Most women would probably never do anything like that. God puts a different gene in the male species that makes them enjoy the above scenario.

And the only reason this female has any idea about it is that The Kid has decided to take up the sport of paintball.

From Nintendo 64 and Sony Play Station, we have now graduated to taking pseudo violence into the woods with guns that look like a cross between an old Super Soaker and a Rube Goldberg sculpture. Instead of bullets, we're using little round paint balls that explode on impact.

The Kid tells us this is a game of strategy and one with myriad rules, depending on who's playing and what mood they're in. You can play for time, or you can impose other conditions that call on the male mind's penchant for strategizing tactics.

The object of any of the games is not to get shot, of course. And the paintball is just a step down in technology from what the big boys in the armed forces use, with their laser guns and vest sensors.

You could probably go into training to play paintball in the real world, including courses on ducking and crawling, covering your partner while he's scrambling to another location, etc. You get the drift. It's the same stuff that's been the subject of movies and books that mainly males enjoy.

There are several catches to this new frenzy that has captivated the juvenile in our house. Catch number one is that sometimes when you get shot with a paintball, it leaves a nasty welt that doesn't go away for days.

Catch number two is that it can be a costly activity. While the costs for equipment have come down since the sport was first introduced, in addition to a gun, paintballs, and CO_2 cartridges, you can invest in extended barrels, high grade paintballs, scopes, and special clothing—not to mention the fees for playing at professional courses. There are paintball courses in the city, one of them in a cave.

The country version of paintball is a little less pretentious— more like little boys playing in the woods, erecting makeshift forts of hay bales to hide behind and shoot each other from.

As a mother I guess I'm okay with it all, as long as he wears his mask and doesn't get an eye full of paint. But, like Margaret in the Dennis the Menace cartoons, I'd like to go along just once to satisfy my curiosity, criticize the whole thing, then come back home to play with dolls. *April 2000*

On being a perpetual embarrassment to your children

Ever since Big Guy was a kindergarten student and the news of a classroom mishap beat him home, he's been grappling with the discomforts of having a mother who operates a weekly newspaper. It's already embarrassing being a male child of any woman, let alone one who writes about all your antics.

Not only do male children have to contend with mothers who have eyes in the backs of their heads and spies everywhere. They also have to put up with someone they now look down on telling them to be sure to wear a jacket and carry an umbrella.

What a six-foot-tall college student doesn't understand is the vivid imagination most mothers possess—an ability to picture your progeny huddled in cold misery, catching pneumonia or worse, on a campus full of unsympathetic souls. Souls that would never dream of baking him cookies or harping at him to wake up and not miss the school bus.

What mothers don't understand is why their male children fight off the fussing in heavy resentment. They don't know we'll continue to worry about them keeping warm and well fed well into our eighties.

And we don't much like it that they fend off our concern with a barely-disguised rolling of the eyes and an exasperated sigh. They don't know we're just doing our jobs.

And what really bothers a mother of a son is how little patience they seem to have for our frailties and failings.

When Big Guy was home for spring break, he made the mistake of sitting in the car to wait for me while I got groceries. He was probably already weary of my having to stop and talk to everyone I knew in the aisles. But seeing me come out the door with the grocery sacker in tow and not remembering where I'd put the car was the last straw. He died a thousand deaths of mortification. His mother was an embarrassing ninny who can't even keep track of her own vehicle.

Naturally, none of this was spoken, but a mother knows all and sees all (or at least pretends to). I had the urge to smack him into the middle of next week or snatch him baldheaded (how about those ancient, quaint colloquialisms?). Just wait until he gets to be 54, tired, forgetful, and achy in the joints. Better yet, wait until he has a teenage or college-age daughter! I sure hope he comes crying to me about how impatient she is with his worrying, or how she gets disgusted when he loses or forgets things. Maybe by that time he'll have his own newspaper column and be able to tell on himself. *April 2003*

The generational gap as applied to cooking and new technology

Having a child as late as age 34, as I did some 28 years ago, leaves a mother open to some gaping holes in the social, business, and political arena. That gap widens when your child is of the opposite sex.

Big Guy has dragged me kicking and screaming into the world of social media and phone texting, although I cannot yet bring myself to type "2" for too and OMG instead of "oh my gosh." But I'm at least sensitive enough to the social mores of the younger generation to know not to intrude on his privacy with something like an actual phone call.

I sent him a text message on his lunch hour today to inform him that we had some used swimming trunks that would fit him and be good for his vacation to the wilds of Wisconsin. I gave him the specs (turquoise and purple) and the label (Adidas), thinking that would be enough to entice him. He asked me to email or send a text with a photo of the clothing, which I finally figured out how to do. He soon replied that the swim trunks were not his style, and besides, he'd been ribbed unmercifully for wearing some blue Hawaiian flowered ones last year on the annual backwoods getaway. I texted a sarcastic reply noting that I didn't realize that Wisconsin was such a fashion mecca and subject to the clothing police, but that's okay. I'll just cart these to Goodwill.

I shouldn't be so harsh. This is the same child who has been helping Lemonade Man and me navigate the treacherous waters of multi-channel marketing that is the new world order facing media types like us. With his encouragement, we're actually attempting things even more complicated than texting.

Last week when Big Guy sent us an email with a link to his new cooking blog, mywifesdiet.com, I realized I'd lost even the small kitchen and cooking advantage I had over him.

Coming from a long line of good cooks, this kid has no choice but to test his kitchen talent. For the past several years he's been treating family members to delectable goodies like his "Skinny Pies" and orange dream cake. His stepdad ruined him for eating steaks anywhere but from the home barbecue grill, while his father made him realize how making a cheesecake is an art form. His new father-in-law is famous for his "butter burgers" on the grill, which Big Guy no doubt will try to emulate. Shoot, his paternal grandmother had to cook for 11 kids and even catered huge meals after The Kids were raised. And his maternal grandmother made the best chocolate meringue pie that ever existed. He grew up drooling over my homemade potato salad and deviled eggs and loved learning how to make "dump cake" before he even got out of high school.

In short, he figuratively burns in the kitchen. I'm the one who does it literally now. His challenge, which led him to the food blog, is pleasing a new wife who is constantly on a diet and has a fairly-limited palate. He makes quick, simple things with unique twists and picks up ideas on their many forays into Kansas City restaurants. The blog is humorous, (could that be something he inherited from me, please Lord?!) in a Generation X kind of way.

The only thing I can do for him at this point, since he didn't want the used swim trunks, is loan him our DVD of "Julie, Julia." Since I'm not aware of anyone writing a blog based on the recipes and life of any famous male chefs, that will have to do for now. *2013*

Part 2:

Laughing at Our Critters

Backstory

I've always had pets, from the time I was able to drag around a barn cat as a toddler, through a series of cats my first husband, Dan, and I had while serving as Peace Corps volunteers. I never knew until just a few years ago that Dan was allergic to cats and I'm hoping that wasn't a subconscious reason he ran over my orange tabby before Michael was born. And he really didn't want the first dog I finally coaxed him to bring home. But by then our son begged for a canine companion.

When I remarried in 1995, I discovered husband Marshall was an animal lover, almost to the point of obsession. We acquired Lhasa-Apso littermates to add to our menagerie of border collie mix Max and two cats. Later, our soft hearts got us accidentally into the animal rescue business, as well as into trouble with all the ways they complicated our lives. And that made for lots of good column material. The columns I wrote about raising pets were almost as popular as the ones about raising a kid.

A message from one of life's great disrupters

The name is Max. I'm a Christmas puppy. The Kid found me in a box under the Christmas tree. Took him about three minutes to name me. Max is such a common doggie name, but (sigh) I guess it'll work.

Training my new owners is hard work. They get super irritated if I miss all the newspapers they have on the kitchen floor. I do it for spite. I don't like being cooped up in one room. I like exploring, eating Christmas ornaments, chewing on the branches of the tree, gnawing on shoelaces, and nipping at hands. My favorite sport is playing tug-o-war with an old sock, followed closely by tearing paper to shreds and chasing a ball.

I'm pretty darn cute and the Mad Mother can't keep from

petting me, especially after she gave me a bath with flea shampoo. Now I smell better.

I've got those intelligent brown doggie eyes that look wiser than they really are. I'm mostly light brown, with a white collar and paws and am developing a dark brown streak all the way down my back.

The Kid wants me to sleep in his bed and have the run of the house. Mad Mother says absolutely not. She wants me in the basement most of the time. Fearless Father doesn't notice me much, but I know he likes me when he rubs my stomach with his stocking feet.

I'm disrupting this household, and boy is it fun. But I'm not all bad. The Mad Mother tells me I make her slow down. She's not used to stopping in her busyness to sit on the floor and play, but now she's the first one that gets to see my wagging tail in the morning (and step in my messes in the dark).

And of course, there's The Kid. He says I'm the best present he's ever had. We're both looking forward to warmer days when we can go outside and run and explore the world and grow up together.

I don't know why this house didn't have a dog before. It's just not too bad a place to hang out. If I can keep from chewing on things like carpets and shoes, I'll probably have a pretty good life. *January 1990*

The battle for peaceful co-existence between traditional enemies: Is there a James Herriott ending here?

We won't lack for entertainment at my house this holiday season. There's a new family member who just took up residence— first in the branches of the Christmas tree and now more or less permanently under a round occasional table, hidden by its tablecloth.

We call her Patches, but maybe it should have been Queen of Sheba. That's more appropriate for someone who's taken over a household.

This innocent little ball of fur landed in the local vet's office after she fell into a vat of white paint and the city police picked her up as a suspected case of rabies. After she was cleaned up, she was right as rain and became a sort of mascot for Dr. Story's staff. Everyone who came in marveled at the sweet kitten, who immediately turned on the purr machine when someone even looked like they were going to pet her.

I fell under her spell when Max went for his neutering. Several weeks later, a spiteful friend who had just gotten a kitten herself, shamed me into adopting Patches for Christmas. Hundreds of poor families needing adoption for the holidays and what do I do? Adopt an orphan cat. What a service to humanity!

But I just couldn't resist that soft fur and those big green eyes. Max sure wishes I had. He's not a happy dog these days.

If I were into reading dog's minds, I'd hear him say, *Why does she get up on your bed when I can't? Why does she wrap herself around your neck when you complain about me getting underfoot? Why does she get to stay in the house all day when I get booted to the garage?*

What can I say, Max? Life's unfair. Besides, cats don't smell. They don't make messes, unless you count all the lower ornaments getting batted off the Christmas tree as a mess. They don't drool, they don't lick your hand, and they don't jump on you and wag their tail furiously.

How can I explain to a poor, dumb dog that a woman likes a cat because they're just like she tends to be—haughty, hard-to-get, finicky, independent, yet very responsive when stroked and fed properly.

The entertainment at our house now comes from watching the dance that a cat and a dog do around each other when they're getting acquainted and when one of them happens to positively hate the other species. *What kind of new live toy is this,* wonders Max, sniffing at her posterior. *Looks an awful lot like a rabbit to me. Wonder if this thing will run like a rabbit?* He chases, cat hisses, spits, and then hides. Max takes up a vigil two feet from her hiding place. Max gets yelled at and sulks away with tail between legs.

Max waits for the proper moment, when I'm picking up Patches, to take a nip at her flank. Max hears a loud "No," feels a swat and finds himself outside. Max doesn't have a good memory. Max spends lots of time outdoors in the rain. Bad dog. Sad dog. He's been dethroned.

But by last night, they were sleeping with their heads about a foot apart and Patches occasionally rubs up against Max for a few split seconds. Does this signal the beginning of harmony and peaceful co-existence? Will they eventually be inseparable buddies? A mother can only hope. *December 1992*

The winter of our pets' discontent

The animals have cabin fever.

Like a crotchety old couple with nothing to do but pick at each other, Max and Patches delight in causing mutual grief on these long, wintry days.

The snow is deeper than Max is tall but that doesn't deter him from running through it like a mad dog, kicking up the white powder with his snout and challenging me to play tug-of-war with a stick. What he needs is a good brisk walk, but I'm one of those criminal pet owners who considers my own comfort first. I'll get my exercise indoors without working up a sweat, somehow. The beast can fend for himself.

Patches, meanwhile, is developing her feline slyness to a fine art. When Max comes bounding in the door, tail wagging, to greet her after being tied up all day, she either runs away and hides under a table and bats at him from under the tablecloth or plops down coyly with her back to him and ignores his playful nips.

She's just as happy for a diversion after a solitary day, but do you think she'd show it?

After the initial "How was your day?" greetings, the dynamic duo turn their attention to getting mine. They follow me from room to room. Patches meows plaintively in the kitchen, sniffing her empty food bowl. If I make the mistake of sitting down for a phone call or a nature call, Patches is purring and sliding around my legs and Max has his nose in my lap, begging to be petted. If their pleas for attention go unheeded, it's not long before Max drops a ball at my feet and gives me one of those brown-eyed pathetic looks, while Patches starts using me as a scratching post.

"What am I, your entertainment center?" I ask them huffily. "No, we're yours," they might as well reply, as I get treated to another episode of "Saturday Night at the Fights" or the four-legged version of the Indy 500. Our long hallway is their racing strip, and my bed is their neutral zone, with Patches on top, reaching for Max below with her deadly claws.

Surely the creator of the Garfield comic strip got his initial inspiration from being cooped up for a long winter with a dog and cat. I think I may have some new material for him. *March 1993*

The impeccable timing of pests ... I mean pets

We animal lovers pay a price for having a slobbering, tail-wagging thing greet us enthusiastically every day and a pile of warm, soft fur to stroke and cuddle up with. I'm referring to our pets' sense of timing.

About twice a week, just as I'm ready to take my breakfast to the table, I hear the noise that I dread ... the sound of a cat heaving. So, before I can eat my breakfast, I get to stack three paper towels together and try not to look as I clean up the bi-weekly hairball. What an appetizer.

The timing thing with pets really hit me full force Sunday night. I'd been on a 1,400-mile trip to Texas to attend a niece's wedding. Got home at 10 p.m. Sunday, all groggy, stiff, and with eyes glazed over from focusing on two lanes of road for the last 120 miles. It hadn't been a good evening anyway. A soft drink had decided to spray all over creation when I opened it in the car, then leaked out slowly the rest of the way. I'd dribbled a juicy burger all over my shirt and didn't realize it until confronted by three highway patrolmen on coffee break at my last restroom stop. And, I'd bucked a strong headwind that threatened to throw my little car off the road.

So, I come into my home with relief and the only thought in my mind was crawling into my own bed. My pets had other ideas. Max greeted me with his usual enthusiasm, but what was that odd smell coming from around his neck? Closer inspection confirmed my suspicions ... he was wearing eau de sheep manure, his favorite thing to roll in. And he wanted to put his face in mine and lick me! Ugh!

The worst was yet to come. The person charged with checking on the cat food and the house had accidentally shut the door to the basement. The basement is where the cat's litter box is. Guess what I found on the bed?

Why do cats do that? And while we're on the subject, why do they choose the moment you're on the telephone to claw the furniture, knead your leg with their paws and claws, and play with the lace tablecloth?

So, instead of falling gratefully into bed Sunday night after a long trip, I got to do laundry and remove sheep manure from a dog's neck.

I guess it could have been worse. A friend's cat had even better timing. She was getting ready for work Monday morning and left the iron on while she was in the shower. Her cat knocked the iron over onto the carpet. The rest of the story involves a trip to the carpet store.

You'd think grown people would be more intelligent than to get hooked up with animals. Especially when their kids get into enough trouble already. *March 1994*

A local version of Charlotte's Web is in production

The American Society for the Prevention of Cruelty to Animals should hire my nieces and nephews.

These children, ranging in age from two to ten, organized a protest in the barnyard last weekend. It all started when Youngest Son and Tallest Son-in-Law decided to really get into the country thing. They went to the livestock market Saturday and came home with ten feeder pigs.

Talk about excited! The offspring of these two men and their assorted nieces and nephews went into frenzied activity. They named each animal. They hovered around the pen, trying to feed the critters grass and leaves. They petted and called to them and squealed with delight at their every movement.

But one of the kids happened to be within earshot when the adults were discussing how good fresh tenderloin was going to taste when the pigs met their fate.

After furtive preparations upstairs, the kids appeared outside. One of the girls was dressed in a pink nightgown with a homemade pig's snout tied to her face. They marched in a line around the pigpen and under the noses of the adults, displaying homemade placards reading, "Pigs are people too. Don't kill pigs," "Don't wrost (roast?) the pigs," "You'll be very sorry, you bad people," and "Butchering pigs is like doing drugs. Keep the pigs."

The unsuspecting animals, now known as Murphy, Piggy, Pinskey, Coco, Spikey B., Spikey S., King Kong, Big Red, Big Black, Snickers, and Babushka Babiyaga Shish Kabob, have already uprooted all the vegetation in their pen. They're oblivious to the stir they've created or to how much they're admired by a bunch of kids. They'll be the center of attention for months, until the time they serve as a lesson in life for some youngsters who will stare at the big people with reproachful eyes and probably refuse to eat pork for the rest of their lives. *May 1994*

Why do they call it 'dog days' instead of 'cat days?'

Dogs are the objects of gross discrimination in this country. When it's miserable outside with heat and humidity, and people are irritable as all-get-out, they name this lovely time of year after us dogs.

You know what I think? It's all because of the way we sweat. Can we help it that we have to perspire by hanging our tongues out of our mouths? God made us that way.

What I want to know is, why they don't call this miserable time Cat Days? After all, cats are the animals that shed all over the place when it's hot. They bite and scratch and ruin the furniture and go wild when the weather's like this. Just now, the visiting cat we have (who won't let me chase him or put his head in my mouth for some reason) got so wild he climbed the fireplace mantel and broke my owner's brass and glass candlestick. And now he's got the couch all torn up where my owner just mended it from resident cat's previous clawing.

So what does she do? She buys both of these creatures a scratching post with catnip in it. This must be the feline version of marijuana, the way they act around it. You don't see dogs doing drugs, do you? Funny thing is, they still use the couch to sharpen their claws.

What really breaks a guy's heart, when he's been so loyal and faithful to his owner, is to see her shower all her attention on these cats. When I come up to her to get some attention, she pushes me away and says, "Leave me alone. It's too hot."

I think it's totally useless that cats don't appear to sweat. They're cool, calm, and collected all the time. And the minute the woman of the house leaves, they start conniving to see what rotten things they can do.

But for all this, I'll bet you wouldn't get a cat to guest-write a newspaper column and relieve a pet owner from the duty because it's too hot to think. So, since I have this forum, I might as well get something out of it. I'm going to declare my own holiday. When it's miserably cold outside and people don't even want to stick their noses out for fear of frostbite, we should declare those days "Cold Cat Days" and kick all cats outdoors.

Now, if anyone is interested in my services as a counterpoint to Garfield, you can reach my agent at 583-2116. –By Max the Wonder-Why-We-Got-Him Dog. *June 1994*

A pet primer for people who aren't exactly posh

Now that it looks like spring has finally arrived, the Mad Mother's household is busy with outdoor projects.

The biggest project currently underway is The Fence. We're talking chain link here, the kind you put a second mortgage on the house for. We picked it up in the pouring rain two weekends ago and finally found someone to install it. If we can keep the kids and balls and dogs off the posts until the concrete dries, we'll be able to protect our investment.

The part that worries us is our motivation for the project in the first place. We're not installing 200 feet of fencing for privacy or beautification. We're doing it because of various four-legged critters.

Lemonade Man is tired of cat prints on his vehicles and trophy mice in his garage. The Kid is tired of yelling at Max-the-Wonder-Why-We-Got-Him dog for barking at people in their own driveways and chasing kids on bicycles. The Mad Mother is done with chasing pups that run into the street and down the block when they're finally let out of the house.

The biggest problem with this expensive project is that it is leading to others. In order to keep the fenced enclosure from becoming a mud hole, we have to put landscaping rock around the foundation of the house. That entails lawn edging and black plastic wrap and a whole lot of labor. Then there's the matter of purchasing a pooper scooper. (I'd like to come up with a more refined name but am at a loss.)

While we're at all this, we figure, why not blow some more money and order some railroad ties for other landscaping projects, then put new gravel on the driveway. Where is it going to end?

Lemonade Man says for all this money, we could have had a hot tub and an above-ground swimming pool. And if, after all this expenditure of time and labor, a critter decides to tunnel his way to freedom, we could have a dead dog.

So, let this be a pet primer for you. When you consider the vet bills, the food bills, the fencing and the destroyed property, don't buy a pet. Buy a hot tub. You'll be able to send your kid to college that way. *April 1996*

The Not-Dead-Yet Rabbit Chronicles

Forget all the warm fuzzies you associate with bunnies. They're not worth all the fuss. At least that's what I'm trying to convince

Lemonade Man.

It's a good thing he never read *Watership Down*, or he'd be even more of a fanatic about kindness to God's beasts. Right now, we have a resident rabbit that has become an obsession with him.

It started this winter when we noticed all the beautiful bushes around our patio were beginning to look a little skimpy around the bottom. No, make that *a lot* skimpy. And every time we let the dogs out in the fenced-in back yard, they got their exercise chasing two rabbits who had apparently set up housekeeping under a garden shed. When the dogs tired of chasing, they went searching for rabbit droppings. They don't just roll in this nasty stuff. They eat it. The vet says all dogs do.

Now, maybe this is part of the recycling nature of the universe, but there's something a little off-putting about having a dog that just ate bunny dung licking your face or your fingers.

The rabbits had to go.

In a seed catalog, we found the answer—a live animal trap.

So, off goes Lemonade Man to Orscheln's to purchase one of the contraptions at about half the cost of the one pictured in the catalog. While there, he was laughed at wryly by a man whose wife had wanted him to do the same thing. She didn't win.

This fellow rabbit sufferer gave my mate some advice. For the garden variety pesky rabbit, he said an old farmer had told him to play a radio on an all-news station at odd times of the day and night and to leave a light trained on the garden during the night. That seemed to keep all varmints out of the vegetable patch, said he.

So, instead of buying chicken wire to go along the electric fence this year, we may buy the cheaper radio and see if that works. But for the closer-to-house variety rabbit, Lemonade Man bought the trap, some hardware cloth and stakes for about $55, then filled his can of diesel. It was time to batten down the hatches and bait the trap.

The hardware cloth took all day to install around the shed. But that came only after he soaked the ground with diesel under the shed, where a maze of rabbit burrows lacked only a traffic light to govern their frequent comings and goings.

The first night of baiting the live trap with carrots and lettuce brought immediate victory. The male rabbit succumbed and was taken in the back of the pickup to a new abode a mile away in the woods. Now, to the lighter and somewhat crippled female.

I've always known the fairer sex was more intelligent. This one refuses to be caught. Every night we try a different technique of trap baiting, tying the carrots in places we're sure will result in springing the latch and catching her. No dice. But the carrots are always gone.

Perhaps this is poetic justice for the owners of the house, whose dogs crippled her in the first place. Now it may be our lot in life to continue furnishing her with carrots, praying she doesn't have any offspring and leaves the darn bushes alone.

I've reminded Lemonade Man that I grew up on rabbit and squirrel stew, with the beasts cooked in marsala wine, spitting out buckshot and being none the worse for it. He reminds me that all we have for that purpose is a .38 loaded with snake shot, which would do more damage to the surroundings than the offending animal. When I suggest loading the gun with a real bullet, he informed me there would be nothing left for stew with that weapon.

Now we're discussing a hired gun or buying a .22. Let's see. That would bring the tab for disposing of one rabbit up to about $300. Then, if we have to resort to the chicken wire remedy, we'll be in the neighborhood of making it more economical to move back to town.

How much would a rabbit-hungry black lab cost? How much food would that big a dog eat? How much of a mess would that dog leave in the yard from his own waste?

I wonder if rabbits can be trained to do tricks other than steal bait from a trap. *April 2003*

Fitness with Fido: Something else to feel guilty about

Our dogs are couch potatoes. While we're at work, these aging canines are curled up on the recliners fast asleep. When they're bored, they get in the trash basket and string tissues all over the house. If we're stupid enough to leave any newspapers or magazines on the floor, they use them as skateboards. Getting in trouble is the main exercise they get.

So, it was with a pang of guilt I read this week that out of 1,000 randomly sampled adults in Australia, those who owned dogs spent less than an hour a week walking their dogs. Some 59 percent said they never walked their dog at all.

This group of researchers claims that if all dog owners walked their pooches 150 minutes a week, most of them would be getting enough exercise to dramatically cut cardiovascular disease, diabetes, and colon cancer. That's not even considering the health benefits for the dogs.

Supposedly, some 60 percent of our dogs are portly. Cardiac arrest claims for pets are up 47 percent, diabetes by 16 percent, and hypertension by 27 percent.

So why, when presented with such evidence of what would be an obvious boost to our health and that of our best friends, don't we get out the leashes right now?

Okay, I'll tell you. Have you ever walked two dogs at the same time? How can any pet owner/walker ever get any exercise when one pooch goes to the field to chase a rabbit and the other wraps herself around your legs with the leash?

We've gone beyond the call of duty when it comes to our daughter dogs. When we moved to our present digs on 15 acres, thinking it would be a great place for canine exercise and adventure, we quickly learned that letting them out to do their business before we're dressed could result in having to head for the woods in robe and slippers.

So, we built a fence around the back yard, giving them half an acre to get in trouble in. They didn't disappoint us. They heard the water running from the septic tank to the laterals, so they tried to dig to China to reach that water. Now we have a bare spot in the lawn that nothing ever grows on.

Not content with that, the two of them have developed a real affinity for rabbit droppings. If rabbit dung is scarce, they'll find moss or something nasty to roll in, then act offended when we refuse to let them snuggle with us in the recliners.

A steep stairway on our deck to the back yard becomes an ice-covered hazard for the dynamic duo, so we let them out the front door in the winter. Now, we get to watch them check out the bird droppings and birdseed hulls under the feeders and worry about bird flu.

Sure, they'd be better off if we walked them every day. So would we. But our vet tells us they'll probably live long lives because they don't have to shiver in a cold outdoor doghouse and because they're not stressed by anything but waiting for us to come home.

Actually, barking may be their best exercise. And they get plenty of that when they stand at the top of the stairs each night, asking us where we've been all day and why we abandoned them for eight hours while they were working so hard at resting.

So, dog owners can't win for losing, but neither do we need to have one more thing to feel guilty about. Maybe we could carry the dogs on our walks, getting the benefits of weightlifting. I'll suggest that to the Australian researchers. *January 2006*

The critters are in control at our house

Last year we began calling him "Pool Boy." He distinguished himself from the other squirrels that scamper busily under our mature white oak trees with the habit of checking out our pool and making it his personal playground.

We kept seeing little muddy pawprints all along the side of the pool and assumed it was another critter, one of our many raccoons, who needed to wash his food before eating. But one afternoon, Lemonade Man came home to find this familiar red rodent with a bushy tail flat on his back, sunning on the diving board. He seemed highly offended that he had to leave his choice spot due to a human trespasser.

At other times he has been caught playing with the water flowing from the slide and getting a good long drink while standing on the top step of the pool. His innate curiosity has led him to climb the steep stairs to our deck, sit on the ledge and look in the atrium doors to find us watching television. He checks out the barbecue grill to see if we've left any choice morsels he may need to store away and seems to love to lick the grease can underneath.

We've put up with his idiosyncrasies, calling them cute, and almost considering him an odd little pet. That is, until last weekend's container gardening project was completed.

After nearly breaking our backs hauling potting soil, filling four whiskey barrels, and converting three stone planters from flowers to vegetables, we came home from work to find the odious rodent had lifted the netting we placed over the planters. He decided he didn't want onion sets in his territory. They went on the patio. The rest of the dirt in all the containers showed definite signs of squirrel digging.

Going for the .22 will be the last resort for a man who brakes the truck for birds and rabbits. So, out comes the live trap and it's baited with corn. A few kernels are scattered in front of and around the wire trap.

Next day, the miscellaneous corn kernels are gone but the trap is not sprung. Pool Boy is no dummy. Matter of fact, we found one of the corn kernels in a planter. Maybe he's thinking of growing his own.

We're reading about folks who have adopted squirrels for pets and taught them to use litter boxes. This one shows signs of being able to pass the ACT with flying colors, so a litterbox should be a breeze. But if we don't have any patio vegetables this summer, I may have to take up target practice. Besides Pool Boy, we have a few gophers to practice on. *April 2006*

This'll teach us to count feet first and not to eavesdrop

When your children have flown the coop, animals sometimes take their places, if not at the table, at least underfoot, somewhat in the heart, and definitely in the billfold.

We were shopping at a mega pet store recently and I spied a pair of doggie booties. Ordinarily this wouldn't capture my attention, but last week's ice storm and the advent of arctic temperatures caused the following scene to unfold at our domicile:

In the course of letting two dogs out to do their business, Alpha dog does okay for about three seconds on the frozen tundra. Then, the paws go up gingerly and she does a jig. Then she keels over with her feet in the air.

Thus, my newfound interest in doggie booties. I waved them in front of Lemonade Man's face and said, "Look at these! They're just $15 and we only have to buy these four for both dogs."

He eyed me with arched eyebrows and said, "How many feet do our dogs have?" Then it hit me that our animals, though they might seem like two-legged critters mentally, actually walk on all fours, so one pair of booties would not do.

We just bought one pair anyway, to see what kind of reaction they'd get. We tried them on the cold-footed one and she walked with one foot held high, then the others in succession, until she got the feel of them. Once outside, she ran around like a crazy woman, testing out her new four-wheel drive tires. It worked just fine, until she executed the move that indicates she's done with her business (scuffing her back feet.) The new boots went flying.

So much for that experiment.

Actually, the dogs have been occupying way too much of our thoughts and conversations lately. The sickly one has been keeping us up at night with her constant scratching and chewing, a manifestation of her lifelong allergies, or perhaps a side effect of her newly-diagnosed diabetes.

We've become creative in our strategies for treating this dog, hoping to prolong her life. Lemonade Man was discussing our new "ambush" method of giving her insulin with friends at a retail store in Cameron this week. He didn't realize a woman at another counter was eavesdropping. He had just launched into a description of how he throws her food bowl on the floor, grabs her by the hip, and puts a frozen washcloth on the injection spot before shooting the insulin in, all before she can figure out what hit her. At that point, the eavesdropper turned around and looked him in the eye and said forcefully, "You brute! How could you possibly treat your wife like that, throwing her food on the floor!"

Lemonade Man sputtered, "My wife?! No, no. I'm talking about my dog!"

The embarrassed woman then suffered her husband chiding, "That'll teach you to eavesdrop!" *December 2006*

Animal behavior is directing idiotic human reactions

If you watch any of the science channels on cable television, you can work yourself into a tizzy of worry. Besides global warming and the potential for killer tsunamis, we're dismayed at the possibility of an F5 tornado that could one day whirl through Dallas at rush hour. Or, how about the disappearance and/or deformities of frogs, or the flying fish and crawling zebra mussels that are getting into waterways they shouldn't? Then we have the specter of the earth's core melting away into nothingness.

We can anticipate the eventual end of the earth as we know it, but probably not in our lifetimes, unless the predictions of our demise according to the Mayan calendar in 2010 are accurate. With all this to occupy our nightmares, about the only thing we can do is worry about our own little corner of the world and how to keep it intact.

It's difficult, especially when you look at animal behavior in your own back yard. This spring, thanks to the late freeze, we were privileged to witness the unusual sight of rose-breasted grosbeaks at our bird feeders, when they normally stick to the treetops on their migration paths. This year also brought a pair of indigo buntings, whose brilliant turquoise plumage stands in sharp contrast to the golden finches. They're all still hungrily beating a path to the feeder, and here it is June. The male finches are especially bellicose this year, flying up in pairs and fighting over who gets a perch, while below, three squirrels, a pair of cardinals, and two doves vie for the cracked corn the wrens peck out of the way and onto the ground.

This year we've moved our hummingbird feeder two times to

keep swarming bees off the deck. They took over the oriole feeder too, at first frequented by as many as eight of the brilliantly-colored feathered friends, so we stopped feeding them, replacing the bright orange nectar holder with a basket of artificial flowers.

Then there was the high water in May that brought a few extra snakes our way, including the black snake that made the mistake of getting too close to the patio door and meeting his demise at the business end of a long-handled ice breaker.

Now rabbits have chewed away nearly all the green bean leaves and robins took advantage of our tender young tomato plants to line their nests, leaving us with stubs and the necessity of replanting with bird netting around the cages.

Yes, the birds and bees and other critters are acting out this year. One poor bird built her nest in the sink of our barbecue grill and just keeps sitting, even after three weeks of no egg laying activity.

Another young bird fell out of its nest while Lemonade Man was mowing. He braked seven inches short of running over it, stopped only by its parents dive-bombing him. Then we watched in amazement as the mother bird tried to coax her young'n onto her back to return to the nest. It wasn't working, so we went in search of nesting materials to hang in a temporary location until the critter got its flying wings. But by the time we returned to the spot it had hopped to, it was gone.

Someone besides the critters knows we're suckers for animal intervention. On Thursday a beautiful white cat appeared at the edge of the woods by the barn. She was apparently hunting and when I called to her, she made no attempt to run away. Saturday morning, as I tried to discover why there were no birds at the feeder and opened the front door, there she was, crying and emaciated with hunger. Being the soft-hearted suckers we were, we fed her from our own stock of cat food and gave her water. Though we have an ad in our free pets column this week, we're probably doomed.

The poor thing is less than a year old and obviously very pregnant. Already she's stuck to Lemonade Man like glue, following him all over the yard, investigating his many chores and nearly tripping him several times. Naturally he compounded the problem by naming her Buttons. All I can do is worry about what strange locale she'll decide to have her family in and how to keep her out of the house and away from the other jealous indoor types. As we went to bed last night, she had already tried to scurry into the front and back doors when they were opened briefly. An owl screeched nearby, followed by a cat scream and a thump. I stayed wide-eyed until 1:30 a.m. thinking she'd met an untimely end.

Over coffee this morning, with a white cat purring on the swing beside us like she belonged there, we discussed the broader implications of all this animal kingdom activity and how it will affect human lives already over-burdened with responsibilities.

We may start wearing signs on our foreheads saying, "Idiots for Animals." Maybe that will make us stand out from the crowd when the end comes. *June 2007*

Preparing a cat maternity ward . . . a dress rehearsal for bigger tasks?

We almost considered sending out birth announcements.

Two days before we intended to deliver our stray to new digs with another family that really wanted a white cat, she foiled our plans by delivering a kitten. We had pictured a whole litter of at least four fluffy little fur balls cavorting around our patio until weaning time, but being a first-time mom, this cat delivered only one.

The maternity ward chosen for this blessed event was the underside of a wooden plank leading up to our garden storage shed. It had already been used by a rabbit last winter, so it had a ready supply of unidentifiable but comfortable birthing debris. Still, there was only about 4" of space to maneuver in, complicated by a large supply of last fall's oak leaves, so it was impossible to see the new cat child.

As we unscrewed the ramp from its ledge and uncovered the maternity ward, we saw a 5" ball of black and white fur with pink feet. Mama Cat, whom we've dubbed "Buttons," was quite nervous until her haven was re-covered. Meanwhile, the news was passed to family members in the city, who vicariously had experienced the advent of this new unwanted pet, urging us to keep it. While we reminded them they weren't the beneficiaries of shedding cat hair or vet bills, they let us know the birth occurred on the Feast of the Sacred Heart, surely making this a Catholic cat. They further suggested the name of Mary Frances in keeping with that denominational bent, but lifting the newborn's tail revealed the inappropriateness of that moniker. Knowing his father by catching glimpses of him in the pastures, we're thinking that "Stud Muffin" might be a better name.

So, for the past week, we've worried about high temperatures baking newborn cat brains. To avoid that, we've tried shading the ramp from the direct sun it usually gets by using a beach umbrella and a folding chair. Neither was too effective. We had already tried to move the new family to a Rubbermaid locker we use to store chair cushions, but she immediately picked up her child and returned it to the ramp. Yet she'd go into the two storage sheds every time we opened the doors, trying to find a new, protective location, away from snakes and other varmints eager to eat her baby.

Last night Lemonade Man pulled out a dog carrier from one of the sheds, removed its wire door, lined it with old sheets, put it inside the previously-mentioned locker and we installed the kitten inside. To further protect mother and son, the lid to the locker was propped open with a beach umbrella pole, then the side door was closed with two screws. A pan of dry cat food and one of water completed the new apartment. To our relief, this new arrangement was acceptable. We stayed outside until well after dark, just to make sure Mama Buttons could jump back inside. When we last saw her, she was purring contentedly and nursing her baby.

Yes, we are nuts. Who else would go through such contortions to make sure that the bird's nest in the barbecue grill had a big enough opening only for a mama bird and not for a hungry cat's paw? Who else would already be scheming about how to fix a pen for a kitten that could easily find himself in a swimming pool?

It's time for us to move back to town or to the city. We can't possibly save all the wild critters that get themselves in trouble or in a family way and happen to land on our 15 acres. In the city we'll probably have to confine ourselves to worrying about homeless and frightened humans. Maybe this animal stuff has just been a rehearsal for bigger needs that God will present us with. *July 2007*

The cats are too much with us this Christmas

C. W. Guswelle, the veteran Kansas City Star personal columnist, often writes about his pets. He's even written an entire book called *The Rufus Chronicles* about his favorite hunting dog. I'm thinking of copying his lead and authoring something like *The Cathouse Chronicles*.

As you've heard here before, we went from one aging feline whose life was sadly terminated, to suddenly three cats, animals whose antics are consuming our energy and causing Lemonade Man and I to fight like cats and dogs.

We're trying hard to understand the subtleties of animal pecking orders. While not exactly pack animals like their dog counterparts, they are still in need of a top dog (make that cat) who can boss the others around and put them in their place when necessary.

We once thought the boss cat was Buttons, the mama who adopted us this spring whilst gestating (which we only realized too late). But being boss requires constant presence and Buttons came to us with wanderlust and shows no signs of disliking travel to distant woods. One morning we noticed blood flowing all over her nice white fur coat and discovered she had taken a puncture wound under the chin from a wood rat or opossum. She was in sick bay for a week while we regularly doused her with antibiotics and alcohol swabs to the wound. She couldn't very well take charge of the other two from a wire pen.

Tony the Wuss was in mourning for his absent mother. He retreated to the cat shed to curl up and pout, refusing to eat or drink or use the litter box. The older, un-neutered male we had rescued from under the shed at our office and eventually tamed to the point of obnoxiousness, was having a great time bouncing around, climbing trees (much to the disgust of declawed Tony) and trying to engage his stepbrother in wrestling matches. Freddy Krueger, as we've dubbed him, had settled in comfortably with the idea of having a constant companion in crime, but the delicate cat balance came undone with the reappearance of Buttons from sick bay. Suddenly, the two males realized there was a female in their midst again and at least one of them was old enough to begin to assert dominance.

The weekend we brought all three of them into the garage to escape the frigid temperatures was a day we'll recall with un-fond memories. Freddy Krueger decided to attack Tony Wuss underneath my new Buick while Lemonade Man was grooming a dog nearby. From upstairs where I'm addressing Christmas cards, I hear a distress call directing me to get down here and find the cats that have crawled into the engine compartment of my car.

What a fiasco! I can't see a single cat tail or paw from my position on the concrete garage floor. I open the hood. No cats. I slam the hood shut, nearly causing Lemonade Man to cut the dog to shreds with the clippers when he jumps in surprise. At his suggestion, I get in the car, back it slowly out of the garage while getting a signal from the car computer that I'm about to run over a child, and park it outside. I go up to the barn to get the car creeper and ease my girth onto it for a look underneath a vehicle that has no right to be made so low to the ground. Still no sign of cats. Suddenly, Freddy Krueger appears at my side, looking for his nemesis too. Lemonade Man joins the hunt, and we discuss taking the car somewhere that has a hoist, wondering if he'll make the ride in the bumper and just how much of the car we'll have to take apart to get to wherever he's hiding. What will the repair bill be, we wonder?

On a hunch, I return to the garage and look behind a 6-foot panel of sheetrock. There's Tony the Wuss.

Things haven't settled down any since that episode. We take pity on our feline friends when it's cold outside and bring them in, only to have them act like normal cats, jumping on furniture, chasing each other madly through the house and eluding our clutches when it's time to go back outside.

Lemonade Man tried to give them to the Culligan Man yesterday. No luck. We've now got a neutering appointment for Freddy Krueger. Perhaps that will even out the political imbalance currently operating. I can only hope they don't knock down the Christmas tree, as the supreme pack leader has threatened to cancel the holiday if that happens. *December 2007*

Take your pick: A party for rescued animals, pampered chefs, or tool toters

We can't decide whether our house could now be considered a zoo or a party house.

We've expanded the number of "livestock" on our mini-farm from two to six in recent weeks. And the house will be the scene of a Pampered Chef party this week, but Lemonade Man is considering approaching Snap-On Tools or Bass Pro with the idea of hosting home-based parties for guys, complete with beer and peanuts and a preview of the latest fishing or mechanical gadgets. He could be on to something.

While we're digesting that million-dollar idea, we're having an animal party every day, twice a day. Besides the two indoor canines, we have two felines ensconced in their own private digs in our garden shed. They've been with us since the mother wandered on the place this spring. Now Buttons and her four-month-old offspring consider themselves part of the family, despite a growling and pouting rejection by the indoor contingent. Still, they sneak into the house every time they're quick enough to spot an open door and skirt the grouchy dogs to engage in wrestling matches in the living room.

In the past week, we took on an unusual dog—a rare African, short-haired breed that was in danger of freezing outdoors this winter where she was tethered. She came with a wild cat, whom she had befriended. We couldn't bear to separate them. So now they're camped out in the barn, waiting for a more permanent home. They've both had trips to the vet, who is beginning to wonder if we're going into competition with the local animal shelter.

Lemonade Man doesn't want anyone to know what a softie he is, so act like you didn't hear this. While he's determined to find good homes for the four extras we've acquired, he's just as bent on making the newbies comfortable. For the barn crew, that has included the purchase of an insulated doghouse, complete with a heated pad. For the cat shed, we're featuring an oil radiator that warms the small building at night, plus a heated pad, plus a cushy bed up on a high shelf where they like to hang out. Our latest shopping excursions to Orscheln's have included an agonized pondering of which pet bowls are most suitable, along with which treats would likely satisfy each individual in our new zoo.

Our morning routine has expanded from giving one dog an insulin shot and feeding her and her sister, to taking a tray of canned cat food to the shed, turning the radiator off and cleaning a litter box there, to a trek to the barn to walk a high-energy dog who will run for the woods and a two-hour exploratory course if you turn your back for a second. The barn cat has to be fed on a shelf to keep the dog from eating his food, while we make sure the cat doesn't eat the dog food on the floor.

Yes, we're certifiably nuts. If I forget something important for this week's Pampered Chef party, I have the excuse of operating a temporary animal shelter. We've both decided that if there is such a thing as cross-species reincarnation, we'd like to come back as our own pets. *2007*

Using a pizza box to get a turtle to the other side of the road

Lemonade Man's compassion for all God's creatures is going to get him killed.

My mate apparently has no consideration for his own safety or well-being where animals are concerned. You've already heard the stories of bird and cat rescues and of kowtowing to domestic animals at the risk of our own health and peace of mind. Well, extend that now to a snapping turtle.

This is turtle mating time, so there are tons of these critters crossing the road to get to a female on the other side. One such specimen, an ancient, huge snapper, crossed our path on the way home from work the other day. I had just noticed it when Lemonade Man pulled over to the side of Highway 69, exited the car, and donned his figurative Good Samaritan cape.

As he approached this ancient reptile, he spied a pizza box abandoned on the shoulder. While Mr. Turtle decides to avoid him by walking down the highway's centerline, Lemonade Man begins herding the behemoth with the box. The snapper grabbed the lid and held on, presumably until lightning struck, but being only cardboard and not a human body part, he let it go to continue his journey. That's when the pizza box became a pry bar, going under his shell and flipping him side to side and end over end until he got to the road shoulder and into the ditch beyond.

While all this is occurring, I'm watching in horror as rush hour traffic on the highway comes from both ways and other drivers see an idiot trying to save a turtle. They stopped, from both directions, thank goodness. One male driver rolled down his window and shouted encouragement, while a female driver going the other way was laughing so hard she almost went into the ditch. But she gave my mate a thumbs-up and clapped her hands in approval. We're just happy that none of the drivers was the kind who would head straight for the clueless reptile in hopes of having some turtle soup. *2008*

The Puppy Chronicles: Second Generation

It's terribly embarrassing to have to admit that we've executed another stupid move, but let's call a spade a spade. In this case, we'll call puppies a mess.

It had been seven months since the sound of a barking dog had echoed through our home. Lemonade Man swore that no animal could ever take the place of his beloved Pepper and Ginger, a/k/a the Spice Girls.

Make room for the Flower Girls—same breed, different colors. We picked up the duo on a cold day in January as they turned eight weeks old. Little puff balls they were, just barely getting their teeth. We thought we could keep them in a large dog pen we had on hand from previous animal rescue days. That lasted a week. Lemonade Man decided they needed to be in the kitchen, with more room to run around and play. Off he goes to the lumber yard to have a special hinged fence made from 2-sided finished plywood.

Good-bye kitchen, hello doggie playpen. Good-bye weekend trips and maybe a cruise, hello dog-sitting. Good-bye new furniture, hello nice couch that's been through other doggie barfing and chewing and several deep steam cleanings. Here we go again in the dog parenting business.

It was only two weeks into the kitchen playpen that we decided we need to let them out of prison occasionally so they could chase the cat and have accidents in the rest of the house. That's when the newly-constructed indoor doggie fence was sawed at the quarter mark, re-hinged, and attached to a small holding pen inside the kitchen so we could walk into the room without nearly breaking our necks by catching a foot on the fence.

We're now in the teething stage, the era that seems to last a year. We got home yesterday to a large souvenir wood chip pried from part of the kitchen baseboard and soaked in dog slobber, indicating an attempt to swallow it whole. Already the kitchen cabinets are peppered with teeth marks, despite the fact the dogs have plenty of chew toys. They like irreplaceable things, like our heels and legs, and pajama bottoms.

Each new development or puppy prank has us looking at each other and asking in unison, "Did our other girls do that?!" We're afraid to research the statistics on older folks falling over their pets and dying or breaking bones.

Of course there is an upside to new puppy parenting. We now have watchdogs again, with growling and barking at every suspicious noise or sight, including the cat using his litter box, the television on in the back bedroom, catching their own reflection in a mirror or door glass. We also have so much entertainment in watching two balls of fur chase each other in circles that we seldom watch cable news anymore. It's also nice to have two live pogo sticks greet us when we come home, genuinely delighted to see us again and full of wet puppy kisses and wagging tails.

Laughter has returned to our house, along with constant cries of "Stop, quit, don't!" *2010*

When dogs and cats and opossums have cabin fever

The slogan of our household is now, "I should have had my head examined."

That statement is used equally by me and by Lemonade Man and applies mainly to our regard for animals and the trouble it gets us in.

Not long ago we brought home the cat that was living under our office, since the building was being moved. We just couldn't bear to abandon the poor thing after feeding it all summer and fall.

For weeks, Boots took up residence under the Mugo pines next to the brick wall on our house. She paid for her vittles by killing two baby rattlesnakes and hunting for moles at night. But then came the cold nights and we agonized about how to shelter her. Down from the barn came a kennel and up to the store we went for a kennel cover. After freaking out from going into a cage (she remembers the ride home in the live animal trap in the back of the pickup), she finally decided the shelter wasn't so bad after all. Besides, we accommodated her even further by putting it up off the ground on a bench, under the carport. We offered room service with a heated water bowl and canned cat food twice a day on china saucers (25 cents apiece at the Dollar Barn). She had it made. But when the temps dropped and snow began to blow, the wire cage with kennel cover was replaced by an insulated doghouse, lined with a dog cushion, and topped off with a heating pad. The only thing Boots required was the swinging door to be removed, because she freaked out at that.

We've been weathering the winter pretty well, just worrying about Boots being lonely outdoors while we're in front of the fire. Meanwhile, an intruder cat has been making appearances from time to time. First, he was on top of the barbecue grill on the upper deck, looking in the back door. He had also been spotted trying to steal a meal from Boots, who seemed inclined to run him off. As we didn't encourage him by feeding him or petting him, we thought he'd found a new sucker somewhere else.

Today, Lemonade Man went home from the office early and called back to report that Boots and Intruder Cat were in the doghouse together. Outside the house, a baby opossum, whom we've seen drinking out of the heated water bowl right outside our back door, was also trying to climb the bench to join the party.

We shouldn't be surprised. One night I almost stumbled on the opossum in the dark and watched him waddle up the driveway and slither into the crack under the barn door. When the last snow fell and the guy came to clean the driveway, we noticed the crack under the barn door was blocked shut. Uh oh! Lemonade Man actually went up the driveway to clean out a hole so the opossum could get back outside. Maybe that's where the intruder has been living too. What a happy little family!

Back at the ranch, the indoor dogs are suffering from cabin fever so much they've been eating the antique cabinet, tearing up their beds, tearing up the inside cat's bed, and puking wood fiber all over. We'd make a rubber room for them, but they'd just eat the rubber.

The only comfort we have is in hearing the weather forecaster say we're halfway through winter. If we have too many more animal incidents, they may all be in the doghouse. *2011*

Part 3:

Laughing at Life in the Singles Lane

Backstory

Sometime during the summer of 1990, Dan and I separated after several months of marriage counseling. I moved to a friend's cabin at Lake Viking, which was a wonderful place to get quiet, journal, and look out the sliding glass door on three sides of the place, through the trees and down to the cove that led to the main part of the lake. Michael found it a great place to explore, go fishing with his buddies, and just hang out with me on the days he wasn't staying with his dad. The little sailboat that Dan had purchased got parked at the lake and one day I foolishly decided to take it out and have a big adventure.

Shortly after Dan and I were officially and amicably divorced, I had purchased a new blue Ford sedan from a Hamilton friend who was a salesman at North Country Ford in Cameron. The impetus for the purchase was the night I came home from Kansas City and the old Volkswagen Golf I had been driving broke down and left me stranded in the middle of a major thunderstorm. Since I was living about 15 miles from the newspaper office, I needed reliable transportation. And now that I was single, I intended to have a lot more fun by meeting girlfriends for lunch in the city. Plus, I had a kid and his dog to transport from the lake to Hamilton.

By 1992, I started looking for a house to purchase in Hamilton so I could save on gas money. I found one at the edge of town that faced a pasture where sheep often roamed. That suited my need for country vistas. And when I started dating again, it provided a little more privacy from prying eyes and wagging tongues when single males came for a visit.

Pee Wee's last summer adventure

You know how you like to pack everything you can think of into that last weekend of summer? For the Mad Mother, alias a female Pee Wee Hermann, it was a wild sailboat ride.

I guess I have a reputation to live up to. When I was five and lived on 20 acres with my family outside Topeka, Kansas, I went for a couple of wild rides on horses. The last ride was over a freshly-oiled road, an adventure that ruined a saddle and got me a bath in kerosene.

You'd think, after age 40, I'd have sense enough not to go off half-cocked and go riding on any untamed thing.

After only one sailing lesson on our little British dinghy, I decided to load up The Kid, Kool-Aid, and Dog and take it for a spin. In addition to Kool-Aid, I was equipped with a trolling motor guaranteed to get me out of tight spot like a lack of wind.

That wasn't the case Saturday. There was plenty of wind. After going in circles in our tight little cove, an adult voice inside me finally said, *Hoist the main sail, dummy, and use the wind instead of some little battery-powered toy!*

But by that time Dog was tangled in the ropes, The Kid was into the Kool-Aid and begging to go swimming instead of sailing, and I was sweating and cussing. I didn't have enough muscle to hoist the mainsail completely to the top and The Kid had pulled the jib sail rope completely off the pulley. So, we sailed very poorly rigged but managed to at least get out of the cove.

The main part of the lake has different breezes. They seemed like gales to a novice sailor.

The Kid wanted me to head to the swimming beach, totally disgusted that I couldn't drive it right to the dock. The disgust changed to fear and lack of confidence in the person who brought him into the world. The second time I tried "coming about," everything inside the boat shifted too far to starboard.

After running over a few swimming buoys, I shakily landed on the beach and let the wind take the mast whatever direction it wanted. Collapsed in a heap on the fiberglass seat, I was grateful for a few minutes of rest. You wouldn't think that holding a rope and a rudder handle and bracing yourself against the side of a boat would be that much work!

By the time The Kid got done swimming, we headed into the main part of the lake in an honest-to-God gale. Clouds were rolling and looking at them made me forget one of the first rules of sailing— don't forget to put your centerboard down.

Consequently, the wind blew us every direction but the one we wanted to go in. Kid was crying to go home by the time I remembered the centerboard. He fell asleep in the bow and didn't get to see my brilliant maneuvering of our craft into our tiny cove. I used some great cross winds to bring her in for a beautiful landing, right where I wanted her.

Upon landing and taking down the sail, my legs were like jelly, my mouth felt full of cotton, and I couldn't believe what I'd just had the stupidity to do by taking my son's life and my dog's life in my own inexperienced hands and the hands of fickle winds. But I plan to do it again if they'll sit still for it. As soon as I buy a book to learn sailing terms and techniques and figure out intellectually what my arms, hands, and legs experienced. *September 1991*

How God punishes FemiNazis and blasphemers

God is punishing me.

He filled my basement with water after I wrote that He doesn't like Northwest Missouri because the rains keep going around us. He's making it so I can't mow my yard or pick my green beans and giving me serious thoughts about the need to search for a book on ark building.

Last night He caught me in a terrific thunderstorm with high winds on the 87th Street entrance ramp to I-435. He must have said, "I'll give her a little nudge to show her who's boss." The nudge was in the form of a five-car fender-bender with me in the lead vehicle. After nearly puking at the thought of another blemish on the new car, I ventured out into the rain and could only detect the smallest of scratches on the lower bumper—in the form of an X to mark the spot.

"Okay, okay, I get the message," I said to the Heavens. "Shall I become an agoraphobic and just keep this thing in the garage and never write any blasphemous columns again?"

The answer that popped into my head was that maybe I could try a little less men-bashing while I was at it.

Actually, Ben Harper gave me that idea. He called to me last week from the cab of his pickup and wanted to know about this activity of men-bashing. He seemed to accept my explanation that it's the same thing that men do when they're together and gossiping. But a country music song says that old men talk about the weather when they're together but old women talk about old men. So, maybe I'm wrong.

Perhaps my biggest sin these days in the men-bashing department has been to repeat a story told by one of my high school classmates who has a rabidly-feminist wife—so rabid that another friend would dub her a FemiNazi.

This woman went to one of those huge building and hardware centers staffed with senior citizen clerks who are always too harried to help. She was buying a ceiling fan or something else that involved some complicated installation. She approached a gray-haired clerk and asked a how-to-question. The man looked at her over his glasses, patted her on the shoulder and said, "Honey, why don't you take this home and have your husband install it for you."

This FemiNazi said sweetly, "Oh, do you need a—(insert the portion of the anatomy that distinguishes male from female) to install this? I thought it might take a Phillips screwdriver."

That's one of the best stories I've heard in ages, but just getting a good laugh out of it probably labels me a FemiNazi. The women I've repeated it to laugh hysterically, while the men just look at me blankly.

Maybe I shouldn't be so open about my opinions. Maybe I should just go home quietly and figure out what to wear to church on Sunday, install my pneumatic door opener (it does take a Phillips screwdriver), and read my Gloria Steinem book ... in the closet ... with a flashlight. *July 15, 1992*

Meet Klutzella, candidate for Guinness Book of World Records, home maintenance division

The only thing that can make a single woman feel more inadequate than home maintenance is parenthood. But this weekend's home chores made me feel like entering my exploits in the *Guinness Book of World Records* for klutziest female.

Thought I'd do a little winterizing on Saturday. I had a whole box of caulking in the basement. After a half-hour search for the caulking gun, I got the ladder situated under the front porch, zealously eyed the cracks where wall meets porch ceiling, and got to work. But no matter how much pressure I applied to that darn trigger, the caulk wouldn't spurt. Naturally I'd positioned it in the gun so that I couldn't read the instructions. Could it be that there was an inner seal, besides the outer one you have to slice off? Yup! That must be the problem.

Down the ladder to search for something long enough to pop it with. A frantic search of the kitchen drawer turned up a barbecue meat fork. That worked, after a fashion, and I was soon in the business of slopping silicone.

The exercise made me admire anyone who can manage to put down a straight bead of plastic goop in a crack without breaking it or without blobbing up the nozzle, and without dripping it all over the wall, and without getting white stuff all over a coat.

The next project for the day involved moving two woodpiles. That's all that was left after a helpful male had used his chainsaw on the remains of a dead tree. My goal was to get smaller size wood to the back porch for kindling in the fireplace and larger logs to the back of a shed for curing.

Now, what does a woman generally do when she doesn't have the proper tools for such a project? She improvises. The Kid's little red wagon became the vehicle that transported two woodpiles to their proper locations.

Do you know how many pieces of wood you can get into a child's wagon? Do you know how many pieces fall off a wagon that travels over bumpy territory? Do you know how hungry you get after that many trips and that much stooping and bending? Would that make a good practical math problem for a college entrance exam?

Since my weekend was showing so much productivity, I decided to take things a step further and shampoo the carpet at one of my businesses. The carpet there is red and pieced in a billion places. It makes you feel dirty just to look at it. That project got underway at 5 p.m. Saturday. It wasn't finished until 6:30 p.m. Sunday.

The machinery of rug shampooing is designed by men to make women look and feel foolish. There are fifty billion cords and connections and hoses, three places where you have to stand on your head to read instructions and fifty billion trips to the sink for dumping dirty water, then refilling and pouring in new shampoo. It's not a project for the weak-kneed. But weak-minded and klutzy will do.

Sure, I read the instructions that said to test a strip of carpet for colorfastness and shrinkage, but who has the time for that baloney? Heck, it took all weekend as it was.

Well, my little red carpet had wool in it. And by golly, wool shrinks when hot water is used on it.

Today, I have a wonderfully clean carpet—one I'd be comfortable sitting or lying on and having clients do the same. But today I also have a carpet that shows every seam and that now has fifty billion tacks to hold it in place.

It was such a wonderful and productive weekend on the home front that I made it even better. The woman who never even puts a butter knife at her child's place setting for fear he'll kill himself put a butcher knife in a sink full of dishwater. Guess what happened? At least I didn't drip any blood on the carpet.

My next big project is a little trim carpentry. I can't decide whether that calls for a jigsaw, a table saw, or just one of those old-fashioned ones powered by arm muscles.

I'm sure glad I have a health insurance policy. I should meet my deductible real soon. *November 1992*

Life lessons learned in a garage sale

In looking at my meager savings account one day, a light bulb came on. I recalled a yard sale I'd had eons ago that brought me a cool $400 in mad money.

Time for a garage sale, said the light bulb. Why do we pay attention to those momentary flashes of insanity?

The closets were soon ransacked for items that never get worn. All those "goal swimsuits" and short sets that somehow never motivated me to lose the necessary inches or pounds went into the garage sale box. And, at age 42, what single woman would ever need all those maternity clothes again?

That dandy little food chopper that I thought would be perfect for an onion never got used. The marketing material that came with it neglected to tell you that it was a pain and a half to wash it and put it back together. That went, as did the anniversary clock that was made of plastic and couldn't be fixed. Nothing was sacred anymore. If it didn't get worn, used, or redeem itself by looking good, out it went to the garage.

The Kid went through the same process with his possessions. All the Ninja Turtles and Fisher Price toys that had outlasted two moves and the biting destruction of a puppy were lovingly labeled with price tags by a boy with dollar signs in his eyes.

All the while we felt virtuous. I was ready to write an editorial about the economic development and recycling qualities of garage sales. On a more personal level, we were simplifying life, getting rid of needless complications in the form of material possessions. It was downright spiritual.

The big day came. The people came a half-hour before it was scheduled to open. They were the veterans, and their purchases were swift and calculated.

Then the rain came. The friend who'd joined her junk with mine to make it a bigger affair sat across from me sighing in impatience. Both of us being Type-A personalities, we didn't even have to verbalize our frustration to each other. We knew we felt exactly the same at being forced to sit still and wait for sales when our yards needed mowing and our houses were crying for Clorox.

The only bright spot came when I sat on my half-eaten donut. I sure flattened that puppy. Our laughter was as much over our own foolishness and waste of time as it was over a flat pastry.

Her take for the day was about $20. Mine was $40. The Kid was relatively satisfied with his $21 but pouted that it could have been more. (He tried to confiscate my price tags and claim them as his, but I was merciless.)

Oh, there were some pluses. Having a garage sale forced me to clean my garage. And now I know that I can save myself a lot of wasted motion. The next time I get in a throwing out mode, I'll go straight to the Salvation Army, or at least to its local equivalent. *June 1993*

A Chevy Chase vacation – single mom style

If you've seen that old Chevy Chase movie *Vacation*, you'd recognize portions of the Mad Mother's trip to Colorado with The Kid, a girlfriend, and her son, The Kid's best buddy.

This was a budget, rent-a-car vacation, the lodging a generous donation of a week's time-share the owner couldn't use and was going to lose. And the gas was a company expense. I had to go all the way to Colorado for fresh column material, see?

We packed enough food to last the week, had all our meals planned down to the last can of corn, and were sweating how to make it to the end with only $200 in cash between us. Food and clothes went on top of the car in a rented bubble. The Kids, a year's worth of toys, games, dot-to-dots, maps, and soft drinks went in the back of the car, and we were off—away from poor flooded Missouri, headed for the drought-plagued West.

We soon discovered there's something about traveling with ten-year-old boys that takes the starch out of you:

• "How many miles now?" repeated fifty-eleven times.

• Toy grappling hooks tossed over into the front seat to snag your hair.

• A Jurassic Park dinosaur scream emitting periodically from the back seat for 950 miles.

• A plea for a pit stop right after you passed the last exit with no more services for 150 miles.

• A choking odor wafting from the back and no one owning up to it.

• Hitting each other a little too hard for "Slugbug" at the sight of a VW.

• Dumping every piece and every card to every game in the floor of the back seat.

• Two bare feet staring you in the face and tickling your ribs while you're trying to negotiate the famously treacherous Wolf Creek Pass.

We made it, despite the questionable entertainment from the back seat. The real fun began today, trying to match energy levels with the boys, beginning at 5:45 a.m. and ending with four changes of clothes, a broken tooth, and a run through the golf course sprinkler system.

They may get to ride in the bubble on the way home. *August 1993*

How a stupid single woman handles roof repairs

The stupidity began Saturday when I put a six-foot stepladder in the soft ground under the eaves of the house. I re-situated it five times to compensate for uneven ground, then climbed to the very top step to survey the chimney and scout for the source of a leak around the fireplace.

I spotted several places where water could get under roof tiles. Back down the ladder I go for the roofing tar, disposable gloves, and a putty knife. Back up the ladder to throw above items and hope they didn't slide back down. Then came a crucial decision.

How do you climb onto a steeply pitched roof when the ladder you have puts you about chest high to the edge? Answer: You look all around the neighborhood, first for help, then to make sure that no one can see you make a complete fool of yourself while grunting aloud, "Think of this as a swimming pool. You're just going to lurch up over the side. All it takes is one little jump."

Before attempting the big lurch, I changed into jeans and a long-sleeved shirt so as not to skin my knees in shorts. It did occur to me to go borrow an extension ladder from a neighbor, but the only one in sight was cussing over a lawnmower that wouldn't start. And I was way too lazy and stubborn to go borrow something. And the jeans gave me confidence. Rather than lurching over the guttering and taking a chance that it would come loose, I hoisted one leg over the gutter.

"Okay, now what?" I wondered, as I found myself extended the entire length of my body, face down on the roof, with the prospects of rolling off a distinct probability. The chimney saved me. I dragged myself up by holding onto it and let the quaking of my innards subside before playing in tar.

Once on top of it, a roof is a fine thing. Tarring done, I walked the length of my house, noting with relief that it wouldn't need to be re-roofed for maybe three years, unless my walking all over it caused leaks. When a bird started dive-bombing me, it was time to exit.

Now where was that darned ladder? Imagine a leg doing 360-degree circles for five minutes in a frantic search for an elusive target. Finally, the leg bone made connections with the ladder bone, and I hugged the ground in giddy relief.

It was only later that I recalled Irston Alden saying when he sold the gallon of tar, "You know that you'll probably have to do this every year, don't you?"

Do hardware stores accept lay-aways on extension ladders?
September 1993

Fall rolls in and the power tools come out

The frogs aren't croaking anymore. Now the crickets dominate night sounds. Even the cicadas have been subdued by the cool weather that presages the change of seasons. Last weekend's cool temperatures lit a fire of ambition, the likes of which hadn't been seen in the Mad Mother since it started raining too much.

With The Kid away for a last summer fling at the lake, I had three luxurious days to myself. Except there wasn't much luxuriating. Saturday found me in the garage, tearing out a piece of sheetrock that had holes in it and replacing it with a new 4x8 sheet.

Too stupid to think I couldn't do something like that on my own, I did just fine, thank you, until it came time to woman-handle that piece of new sheetrock. It was leaning up against the garage wall and needed to have about six inches trimmed off the eight-foot side. For some unknown reason, I chose the bottom side to cut off, then groveled in garage dirt, using the utility knife and a straight edge. Halfway through, it struck me that it would have been a heckuva lot easier to trim the upper side. Then it occurred to me that this was the way to learn household repair—by making mistakes.

The most trying part of that little change-of-season job was getting a heavy piece of sheetrock where it was supposed to go. Morgan Millikan had made it seem so easy when he hefted it over his head to deliver it to the garage. So, why wasn't it budging for me?

Home repairwomen are nothing if not ingenious. The sheetrock got tipped end over end into place, then propped up with a ladder. The hard part was over. The fun part was using the drill, trying to find studs, and driving in the sheetrock screws just far enough to create a little dimple that would be filled in with mud.

The rest of the day was spent with a wide putty knife, a can of joint compound and joint tape, while stationed on a ladder. The next day was devoted to an entertaining shopping excursion.

Instead of looking at clothes and frivolous women things, I went straight to the tool section. Picked me up a tool caddy and my very own Black and Decker finish sander. I'm set now. I have all my screwdrivers and pliers organized, with my very own tape measure and finish sander. Nothing can stop me now. *September 8, 1993*

The frustrating search for a decent hard surface

All of my friends have a sport they're passionate about. One is an avid fly fisherman and dreams of being a fishing guide in Montana. Another one likes kayaking and mountain biking. Still others are into sand volleyball and golf.

I felt real left out until a few weeks ago when I got my very own pair of roller blades.

I picked this sport out of a women's magazine. The article made it sound like I could literally fly on these new-fangled skates. It boasted that the fastest growing sport in the U.S. was better exercise than running, and a lot less stressful on your joints.

Imagine a 40-something overweight female donning a pair of rubber shoes with four rubber rollers underneath, hanging on for dear life to the waist of a salesman and trying to skate on a store carpet and you'll get the picture of the agony and embarrassment that accompanied my first attempt to get passionate about a sport. The helpful salesclerk assured me that he'd sold a pair to a 73-year-old woman who came back later to demonstrate her skating skills.

It didn't even occur to me until I got home with my shiny new Blade Runners and a pair of wrist guards that in Hamilton, Missouri there's no place to skate. Until next summer when the new sales tax proceeds beef up the street department budget, the roads around here will be full of potholes and rocks. Rocks and roller blades don't mix.

If you're ever searching for a hard surface in this town, let me speed your search. There are two suitable places—the concrete apron in front of the grandstand and the tennis court. Both these places, while smooth and great for roller blading, have their disadvantages.

The stadium concrete provides a real challenge for the skater, who has to dodge discarded sucker sticks, already-been-chewed gum, paper cups, and wooly worms. Depending on the timing of your workout, you might have an audience of coaches or Legionnaires/bingo players. My dog was my audience ... once.

The tennis court is equally daunting with its rocks, cracks, and tree debris. But hey, in rural Missouri, we make do. Now every time I go out of town, I'm scouting out possible places to practice this new sport. The Plaza around the famous fountain looks good, and the Missouri Western parking lots have great surfaces. The Watkins Mill hiking/biking trail might even be a challenge. Anyway, they'll be good excuses for a couple of road trips.

Another challenge for the older skater is keeping your kid off your skates. It's turning out to be an expensive sport, since I had to buy him a pair of his own blades. When his friend comes over and they want to skate in the basement, somebody still has to use my blades. Except now this little friend has his own skates and his mother doesn't appreciate me very much.

I almost advertised my roller blades for sale upon discovering that Marilyn Quayle is an avid aficionado of blading. I hadn't intended to pick such a Republican sport.

Despite such tribulations, when I clamp on those skates, fasten the Velcro wrist guards, slap a Kenny G tape in the old Walkman, and start gliding along, it does feel like flying. Reality only sets in when I find myself hugging the ground or a stadium seat. *October 1993*

The art of moving 500 lb. killer pianos

We keepers of homes try out furniture positions like we try on clothes. Only thing is, clothes don't weigh 200 pounds per item.

When the sun came out last weekend, it illuminated the ceiling cobwebs and the dust bunnies in the corners. Too bad the sun didn't show up the cobwebs in the brain. Because when you get in a cleaning mood, mental ambitions far outweigh the capability of a 44-year-old body.

This cleaner warrior in my head decided nothing less would do than rearranging the entire house. Men that I know would grow a beard for something different to do to get through the winter. But women like me have to give themselves new vistas, especially if they can't afford a trip to the Bahamas.

It started innocently enough with a dust rag on the top rung of a bookshelf that hadn't seen any action since it was put in place almost two years ago. Next thought—*I wonder what this would look like over in that corner?* The moment of insanity is when action follows thought.

There's only so much a woman can do with furniture in the

early-attic style. But that didn't stop me from having the couch in four different places. Or from moving the piano—all 500 pounds of it—by myself. In typical independent woman style, I tugged and pushed, asking myself periodically why the thing wouldn't budge even though it had little wheels on the legs. I finally tried pushing with legs instead of arms and upper back.

This single woman has belatedly discovered backs aren't designed for solo piano moving. I've also learned that the Monday after a furniture rearranging weekend is one for the *Guinness Book of Bad Records*. The bacon burned, the cat clawed the couch that was now so much easier to get to, and The Kid knocked over an entire bowl of cereal onto a fresh-scrubbed floor and his clean clothes. He was late to school, I was late to work, and the day went downhill from there. The next day's highlight was a visit to my chiropractor and a few hours of missed work from a backache-induced migraine.

The next time I get ready to move my piano, I'll get help from the girlfriend who shoved her ex's recliner down the basement stairs. *February 9, 1994*

If you long for adventure, avoid the "singles jungle"

Last Saturday, a single girlfriend and I summoned all the courage of our 44 years on Earth and went to one of the popular city night spots for singles to see what happens at these places.

We left our purses locked in the trunk and put our money and car keys in our jean's pockets. Once inside, we grabbed a booth along the perimeter of the joint and started looking around. There wasn't much going on, so we grabbed a basket of popcorn and a club soda and caught up on each other's lives. While in earnest conversation about kids and careers we noticed a table with two men surreptitiously eyeing us. They'd turn their bodies around completely to look our way, then when they caught us looking back, their eyes drifted quickly over our heads to the window above us. Guy #1 was okay looking, if you like rumpled flannel, beer bellies, and alligator cowboy boots. Guy #2 was all in black, 5'5 tall, and weighed close to 300 pounds. Both had the look of being recently released from a mental hospital.

We spent the rest of the evening dreading that those two would be the only ones to ask us to dance. Those fears proved unfounded, however, as they weren't into dancing, just ogling. Instead, a retired firefighter asked Vicki to dance, and I sat alone for most of the evening, getting a complex, wondering whether my deodorant had quit working or whether my face said, "Don't you dare come near me or I'll knock your block off."

Finally, an olive-skinned man with a lot of miles on his face asked me to dance. He was Hawaiian and a chef at the Woodlands. Meanwhile, Vicki had switched from the retired fireman to a younger guy, who was also foregoing alcohol for the evening, and worked with handicapped patients at a city hospital.

My next foray onto the dance floor was with a non-communicative type who just wanted to get close to the pink Cadillac, where the disc jockey was spinning tunes, and dance his fool head off. At least I got some exercise.

I met a contractor and a food broker and had nice talks. Vicki and I both danced with several grandfathers. We enjoyed the music because it was almost as old as we are. We observed lots of human nature and learned that these places were horrible for men, unless they're into rejection. One poor guy had asked every woman in the place to dance and had been turned down by all but Vicki. (Our mothers raised us to be polite, even when we don't feel like it.)

We were just about to congratulate ourselves on our adventurous, educational night and head for home when the Hawaiian reappeared at our table, poured himself his 23rd beer (over ice, no less) and asked me to marry him and let him take me to Hawaii.

That was our cue to make a hasty exit. We drove to the nearest waffle house, stuffed our faces, heaved a sigh of relief, realized we smelled like a cigarette factory, and decided to take up something safer as single women. Like learning to line dance in the safety of our own living rooms. *March 1994*

An utterly cute little tool for the semi-serious gardener

When you're born and raised in the country, dirt grows figuratively under your fingernails, even when you don't work in it. That must explain why many of us attempt a vegetable garden, even when our results are less than adequate.

Last year I watched my tomatoes rot from too much rain. The rabbits ate the beets, and I was lucky to get one mess of green beans. Believe it or not, even the zucchini last year was a flop.

You'd think I'd learn and just give up on seeking a green thumb consolation prize. But there I was last night, planting vegetables under the threat of a severe thunderstorm, forsaking supper and supervising The Kid's homework, all on the off chance that in a month or two I'll be able to pull a radish for a salad and beat the rabbits to a mess of beets.

The old timers would say I'm not serious enough about it. The garden is, after all, only as long as my house is wide. And I couldn't even lie down in it sideways without my feet sticking out onto the grass. And I'm short.

Once again, my rows are crooked this year. And if a gully-washer comes along, I'll be saying, "Bye, bye beans." The runoff from an adjacent alleyway comes through the plot.

But I did get a little more serious about the whole gardening thing this year. Tired of waiting for a relative to come and till, and too un-ambitious and cheap to hire someone else to do it, I bought a new power tool.

It's called a cultivator. It features a two-cycle engine with a choke and a spark plug wire that you can disconnect. You need three hands to start it, but when you do, look out Martha! It goes lickety-split. In fact, you gotta hold that sucker back before it eats up your entire yard with its voracious appetite. But for all that, it won't require a visit to the chiropractor the next day.

The thing that sold me on it was its size and cuteness. Unlike its big hog cousin, the full-size tiller, this little tyke doesn't have to be loaded in a pickup truck to transport. It'll fit into a trunk or even a back seat. And once you start it, you don't have to weigh 250 pounds to keep it in place. If you get mad at it for not starting, it won't kill your foot when you kick it.

It's the perfect power tool for the semi-serious gardener and people who like to play in flowerbeds. After I bought it, I started thinking about all the things I could have better spent the money on. But who needs groceries when you can own a cute little cultivator and not have to rely on somebody else for garden handouts? *April 27, 1994*

Confessions of a power tool weenie

For months now, the Mad Mother has been coveting a chainsaw. It's the only power tool left to place in my single woman's arsenal.

On my last foray into the male world of things that go buzz and require neck injuries to start, I bought a weed chomper (if I'd called it by its real name, I'd have to use one of those trademark symbols). But even as I bought something to trim weeds with, I was drooling over the chainsaws.

With one of those dudes, I could get rid of that ridiculous row of trees that always interferes with my grapevines and raspberries. *Heck, I might even cut me some wood for the fireplace,* thinks I, while hefting one of the models, just to get the feel of it.

"Hey, have you got a lady chainsaw?" I asked the hardware store owner. He made what for him was a guffaw but was actually a little chuckle and pointed me to the lightest model. *It was still heavy,* I thought. I put it down wistfully, after eyeing the price tag, and vowed to have one of them someday. Meanwhile, John Catron is in the store watching all this, and helpfully advises, "You don't need a chainsaw. You just need a man to operate one." I left the store mumbling about male chauvinists.

But Catron's words were prophetic. Enter the biggest ice storm of the century. My trees were a mess. I had a part-time man to operate a chainsaw, but no chainsaw. It was a Sunday. I was going Christmas shopping anyway, so I was advised to check on chainsaws at the Tim Allen store.

Well, the Tim Allen store was sold out of chainsaws, except for this really cute electric jobbie. I fell in love with it. Gosh, it just weighs five pounds and the only thing to remember is to pump the oil to the chain. Course, I had to buy a 100-foot cord to go with it, and naturally that wasn't on sale. Then there was a quart of chain oil to add.

I came back home and the part-time male took in my beaming, self-satisfied look and said, "You didn't buy an electric chainsaw, did you?"

"But it's so cute and so light," I began, but was cut off by a lecture on buying weenie power tools. I was asked to solve the practical math problem of how long an extension cord I'd need to go to the woods and cut logs for the fireplace.

The cute little saw is going back to the Tim Allen store, along with its 100-foot umbilical cord. I guess if I ever need a symbol of female independence (from everything but electricity), I'll know where to find it again. And to tell the truth, I'm a little relieved not to have to face the challenge of the words that came with the saw, "Some assembly required." *December 14, 1994*

Part 4:

Laughing at and with Lemonade Man and the Whole Mars vs.Venus Thing

Backstory

Dean Hughson felt sorry for me. He was running one of the first ever online chat groups for divorced men and fixed me up with a newly-single guy who lived in Overland Park. The man looked like a famous TV news commentator, and we quickly became enamored with each other. A little too quickly as it turned out. Because in a few short months the guy had decided to move back to his hometown of Chicago.

That's when Dean took it on himself to run an ad in the Kansas City Star's personal columns for me. It mentioned that I had my own business and a young son and that I was seeking a friend to spend quiet evenings with in the country. It asked respondents to send a self-addressed, stamped envelope with a letter of introduction and a photo to a blind box. I got maybe six responses but the one that caught my eye was printed with a laser printer on some beautiful stationery. I responded and we met at Perkins in Liberty for coffee. When I first spotted Marshall sitting on the brick wall outside of Perkins, he was wearing cowboy boots, a western tweed jacket, a bolo tie, and a brown cowboy hat. When he stood up to shake my hand in greeting, he was shorter than me. I had to stifle a laugh. But as the evening progressed, the laughter was no longer stifled. It fell out of me, because this man was so funny and so cute. I needed more laughter in my life.

He moved into my house on the edge of town several months later. We got married in July of 1995. He also moved into my office and became the newspaper's Chief Financial Officer, bringing his graphic arts talents and his skills at computer training. As we later discovered, having a husband and wife working in the same office put a strain on the relationship. While we had much in common, we also had a lot we didn't agree on. The red foam brick that some advertising specialty company had dropped off at the office got used frequently as we threw it at each other across the shared office space. We argued a lot about the business. But he taught me and the employees a lot. We also argued about his traditional views of the roles men and women should assume.

In the next 21 years, my second husband would also teach me a lot about home and car maintenance and repair, as well as a deep spirituality, but not at the same time. We learned not to wallpaper together.

Confessions of a left-brain lamebrain

Thank God not all of a mother's sins get visited upon her children.

The Kid came home from school the other day bragging about how he just loved doing word problems in math. He even went into a detailed (boring) description of how he reasoned through the problems. He admitted, though, with some concern, that some of the girls in the class were so upset because they couldn't figure out the problems they were on the verge of tears.

I know exactly how they felt.

It was in the last quarter of my eighth-grade term when I transferred from Raytown South to Grandview. My first day in the new school I was confronted by a terror that went by the name of Mrs. Bandy. They were doing new math in her class. I had no idea how to do the problems. For my ignorance, I was rapped sharply on my knuckles with a ruler.

The next year, I sat in the front row of a freshman algebra class with an impossible crush on the male teacher. That, despite the fact he called me Charlie Brown. I was hopeless at algebra.

Geometry in tenth grade wasn't so bad. I had a female, patient teacher. Besides, all those angles and triangles and circles were at least something concrete. And I could memorize rules with the best of them. I just couldn't play Mickey Mouse games with As and Bs in parentheses.

Word problems? Well, they inspired fear and instilled the certainty that I could never follow the tricky labyrinth to arrive at the correct answer. There must have been word problems on the ACT that I took to get into college. I blocked them from memory. Then I blocked the possibility of ever taking a math class during four years of college.

So, how does a math phobia affect your life? It makes you leave things like handling money and financial planning to a spouse. Big mistake!

At the ripe old age of past-forty, I've been taking a math review course. The old feelings of panic and tearfulness often threaten to erupt in these sessions. But numbers are losing their terror for me. They're being de-mystified. Suddenly, those As and Bs are not so intimidating. Numbers are nice because they're predictable and precise. They don't get subjected to exceptions like English does.

I'm even learning that word problems, while tricky, can be tackled by a grid or a diagram and re-reading the sentence. The thing you don't want to do with numbers is apply your female intuition to them. They don't know intuition. They dwell in the right-brain quadrant of the human, which is home base for most males.

Somebody should let those girls in The Kid's class know they shouldn't be intimidated by a paragraph of words and numbers. They need to know that the problems themselves don't amount to a hill of beans in the scheme of life, but the negative emotions they elicit might stay with you for a lifetime.

Meanwhile, I need to figure out a way to let my male child realize that the savings account he opened two weeks ago should stay in the bank and not be spent on a Super Soaker 100. He also needs to understand that his savings does not double from accrued interest in a few weeks. Maybe I just need to put it all in the form of a word problem. *(1989)*

Waxing cars must be a guy thing

It would never have entered this thick female skull that the thing to do on an autumn weekend is wax your car and get it ready to take on winter's ice, snow, and salt-soaked roads.

Go ahead. Accuse me of gross generalizations and female

chauvinism. But to most women, a car is something to get you from Point A to Point B. Who cares whether there is tar on it from two years ago? What difference does it make that the dash has never been blessed with a coat of Armor All since it left the factory? And does it really matter, in the grand scheme of life, that the tires have never been "dressed" with that whitewall stuff?

To a male, all of the above is important. Grumbling, I spent a beautiful Sunday inside my garage, on my knees on the concrete, with a rag soaked in gasoline, removing tar. Then I got on a stool and waxed the top of my blue buggy.

I would have preferred being in an apple orchard or walking through the changing autumn woods, or watching some relatives slaughter a hog and pretend they knew what they were doing. But no, I got to help wax my car.

I watched a male lovingly caress the clear-coated metal with a soft rag, then burst with pride as the shiny parts came to life again. A woman should get this much attention.

I have to admit, I didn't fully appreciate the gesture of having a friend pay so much attention to my vehicle until I pulled up to the post office this morning and two people asked me if I had a new car. Then one of the questioners said wistfully she wished hers was waxed for the winter. Then she told me how much it costs to have the process done at a detail shop.

I am now a convert to the religion of car waxing. And no, I won't help you wax yours. Once every three years is enough for me.
October 1994

Our Christmas wish: A toilet that won't overflow

All we wanted for Christmas at the office this year we already got. The plumber came yesterday and fixed the toilet.

For about a month now we've been bending over to turn the shutoff valve on the dern thing so the water wouldn't run into it constantly. When it was fixed, we asked the plumber what the problem was and he just mumbled, "It's fixed." It took him three minutes.

Now why, in this office of intelligent females, could none of us do what he did?

The answer is that we could easily have done it. We would just need to decide that we could allocate the time for it and then not panic when confronted with the unfamiliar interior workings of your standard toilet tank. We chose, instead, to call an expert, and for that, we will pay. That's life in this increasingly-specialized society we live in.

And, since we're really into gross generalizations, let's go a step further. This little story has some other universal applications. It leads me to speculate that in our home economics curriculums we may need to add things like elementary toilet repair to the checkbook-balancing, potholder sewing, cooking, things we offer these days for males and females. It is, after all, just as important for girls to know what the inside of a toilet and the backside of an electrical outlet look like as it is for boys to know how to cook.

This theory comes from someone who has become increasingly self-sufficient at home. So much so that my Christmas want list looks like it came from a Sears circular. I ruefully recall the year I was disdainful of receiving something as unromantic as an iron skillet under the Christmas tree. I thought sweaters and jewelry were more suitable.

But this year I'd be perfectly content with an aluminum extension ladder, two window well covers, a cordless screwdriver, a rechargeable flashlight, a three-speed reversible drill, a table saw, a box of sandpaper, a wheelbarrow, and a socket set.

And, dear Santa, wherever you are, I'd like to suggest a perfect stocking stuffer for me and all the other females trying to be self-sufficient: a handbook of elementary toilet repairs. *1994*

All it took to win me over was a tiller and a few power tools

The editor/publisher is going public this week. Time to talk about an addition to life that isn't common at age 45. It's called a fiancé.

This one came with a tiller and his own power tools. He also came with an attitude. He says it's a woman's job to run the house and the man's supposed to mow the yard, change the oil, and fix things.

After struggling through single life for three years, buying my own power tools, and making a valiant attempt at using them, it's a relief to have somebody around that has the muscle to drive a nail without having to visit a chiropractor the next day.

What a deal to have the garage cleaned, the basement organized, closets fixed and expanded, walls painted, leaky toilets repaired, and the car washed regularly.

No, you're not reading the wrong column. The original bleeding-heart women's libber is quite content to accept her allotted role in life as a female who's better at buying and arranging furniture than fixing it. And who likes going through cookbooks instead of trying to start some dumb gasoline machine with a pull starter.

You do what you're forced to do. I've cleaned gutters, caulked leaks, and mowed lawns until I thought I'd croak. The prospects of having someone else do that and let me clean bathrooms is not half-bad.

No, this man is not available for hire. When he's not spending weekends fixing things, he's making me and The Kid laugh and trying to win the affection of the cat, having already scored high with the dog.

Now my biggest challenge is getting motivated to go to work when I just want to stay home and enjoy not having to look at 20 things that need repaired. That, and trying to figure out when the fiancé, alias handyman, will start full time. *April 5, 1995*

The Capital has nothing on us in the battle of sexes

The battle of the sexes is heating up, if you can believe *Time* magazine. Apparently for the first time, we're seeing a huge split in philosophy between men and women about politics. These days the overwhelming majority of women consider themselves Democrats, while the majority of white, middle-aged, middle-class men are staunchly in the Republican camp.

As the politicians and pundits ponder this sweeping tide of potential votes and how to manipulate them to their own narrow advantages, the battle of the sexes takes a different form in the Mad Mother's house.

Here we split on whether to grow a beard or not to grow a beard (the beard question applies to Lemonade Man, not to me—yet). Many wives are thankful their mates have hair there at least, since they have none on their heads. But the Mad Mother prefers the clean-cut look, even though Lemonade Man does grow a cute little goatee and keeps it impeccably groomed. I had been campaigning for a compromise—smooth in the summer and a beard in the winter.

Saturday morning, as we drank coffee on the patio and tried to decide what to do with the gift of a day of less than 100 degrees, he turned full face and asked, "Which side of my face do you like the best?" When my answer was the left side, he smiled smugly and said, "Okay, dear," leaving me to wonder at his sanity.

A few minutes later he was back on the patio, humming and pretending not to be the original Cheshire cat. It took me a few minutes to notice something asymmetrical about him. When I refused to take the bait, he prodded, "Don't you notice anything different about me?" That's when I finally saw that his three-day growth, the one he thought would eventually turn into a beard, was half-gone.

"This side is yours," he said with a look of self-satisfaction, pointing to the smooth-shaven area. "I decided not to mess with the mustache. I've had that too many years."

All day I thought he'd relent and finish shaving. He didn't. By nightfall, I was hoping no company would drop by unannounced and trying to figure out how to explain my husband's idiosyncrasies to the public if I ever decided to accompany him again in the outside world.

I had just about decided to cut half my hair short and leave the other half long in retaliation when he appeared for supper with a smooth chin. To explain his change of face, Lemonade Man said he had to try out a new razor that came in the mail.

If only pollsters and politicians realized how seriously this power play is being waged in the hinterlands. It makes Washington's hullabaloo seem insignificant and petty. *August 23, 1995*

Confessions of a soon-to-be-former slob

I've gone and done something I swore I'd never do—married a man neater and fussier than I am.

My past lifestyle has reserved the chair in the bedroom for putting clothes on that you might wear again but you don't want to hang up with the cleaner clothes in the closet.

This lifestyle also allows the books and magazines and junk mail to pile up on the dryer until you can't get to the lint cleaner.

My laid-back home life, dictated by the fact that I really live at the office, allows for three pairs of shoes in the bedroom and one in the living room, wherever I step out of them. I haven't ever worried about splashes of water in the bathroom sink or how the toothpaste tube is squeezed.

Taking his cues from me, The Kid thinks his bedroom floor is the place for dirty clothes and the bathroom floor the best resting place for wet towels. He thinks dirty socks make the neatest donuts if you roll them down all the way, which the washer and dryer later have issues with.

And of course, we have the garage and basement, which to us were always places to put things we didn't know what to do with. If these areas got swept, it was during a fit of excess energy or anger, when a bit of therapy was called for.

Our lives have changed drastically. Enter a man with the motto, "A place for everything and everything in its place." This is a man who cleans the car once a week, whether it needs it or not. Who sweeps the garage and cleans his paintbrushes until they look like new. Who takes his five-year-old laser printer to the computer shop for repair and is told it looks like new. Who squeezes the toothpaste tube from the bottom and gives the evil eye to those who don't. Who moved in with stacks of coasters that he's placed strategically on every hard surface likely to be a repository for a glass (he forgot the portable CD player though, much to his chagrin).

The man in our house is training us well. After the bathroom sink is used, it's now wiped clean of splashes with a hand towel. Occasionally the bedroom chair is clear enough that someone can actually sit in it. And seldom does a wet towel reach the bathroom floor.

I knew my slob days were almost over last night when the man of the house congratulated me for standing up over a trash can to brush graham cracker crumbs off myself instead of brushing them on the floor.

Now if he could only train the cat to clean her own litter box and the fish to clean their own aquarium.

Meanwhile, our house is a much neater, more enjoyable space, even though we fall off the wagon occasionally and squeeze the toothpaste tube in the middle, just for spite. *November 1, 1995*

Zen and the art of lawnmower maintenance

This weekend I got to watch a master at work and didn't even have to pay for it, unless you count fixing supper as compensation.

Lemonade Man inherited a fanatic's attention to small engine maintenance from his father, who made him crawl under machines and hold up transmissions, etc., while he worked on them. My husband resented the heck out of being made to help fix things when other kids were out playing and riding bikes. But today, he's thankful.

As I watched the master home mechanic at work on the lawnmowers and weed whackers on Sunday, I recalled watching my stepfather work on automobiles and occasionally being privileged enough to be asked to go get a socket wrench. But being a girl qualified me mostly to go on wild goose chases for things like "board stretchers" and then being laughed at for being too dumb to know there was no such thing.

Yesterday, I got to enter a little deeper into the privileged circle of men and their machines. I watched in awe as a foam air filter was carefully taken apart and soaked in gasoline and wondered why no one had taught me to do that before the push mower almost conked out from not being cleaned. Could it have something to do with my dislike of reading maintenance manuals or just the fact that upon reading them and encountering jargon like "zert," I just gave up in frustration.

How is an uninitiated, non-manual-reading-woman to know that eventually lawnmower blades get dull and no longer cut grass? I'm sure I would have called Donnie Rice to come and pick it up and take care of it for me.

We live in a world of specialists (which is no earth-shattering revelation) but there is a downside to this. As I watched my husband get the lawn equipment ready for another season, I wondered what it is about these chores that immediately puts most of us on the defensive, thinking we're incapable of performing them.

There's not all that much mystery or mastery involved in getting a pry bar out to attack a stubborn oil cap. It's not all that hard to put a little jack under a power mower so you can get to the blades and take them off for sharpening. It's actually kind of fun to pull out a diamond file and watch a sharper edge take shape on a piece of metal that's squeezed into a vise and then putting a final edge on it with a bench grinder.

The ritual of lawnmower maintenance is almost complete. I didn't have to do anything but hand over a few socket wrenches and dispose of the oily paper towels and bring the mechanic a glass of iced tea. But if I had to do it next year, I might be able to pull it off. It's no longer assigned to that mysterious realm of "Boys and Men Only" things.

The other conclusion I came to in this philosophical Sunday is that I want my son to learn these things. If I had a daughter, I'd want her to learn the same things.

That led to the memory of days when every car owner was able to work on his own vehicle and his sons and some daughters watched them in fascination. Learning took place in those sessions and camaraderie grew while you leaned on a car's fender and peered into the innards of a carburetor.

What do fathers and mothers teach their children these days? What work do they do together? Is the lesson in life now, "Go find someone who's a specialist to do these chores so you can get back to your computer?" *April 24, 1996*

Wallpapering is not recommended for marriage therapy

When it comes to wallpapering together, women are from Venus and men are from another galaxy. In fact, this issue is too fraught with comedy to ignore it.

Four years ago, before an engagement ring had even passed over my left third finger, my mate to-be had the courage to wallpaper a half bath in the house. He must have gritted his teeth a thousand times, but he was nice about the job. He only sighed a few times. Now, with three years of marriage under his belt, it was Katie-bar-the-door!

The first night, we stupidly started the project at 8:30, just a half hour after I got home from work. We've all been told not to go to the grocery store when you're hungry. The admonition to not wallpaper when you're tired should be added.

For four months, the kitchen has been a dingy, dreary room. Wallpaper was lying in wait in the dining room and had been since April when I got on a Sunday afternoon tear and attacked the walls with a putty knife. On another Sunday, I got out the Spackle and sandpaper and was ready to get more of the job done when Lemonade Man whined that he'd get the walls done another time. I needed to come and watch some mini-series on TV instead. Fine by me.

The only thing that dragged us out of our procrastination was an impending visit by in-laws. Suddenly, Lemonade Man wanted the kitchen done. I saw no need to impress my mother, but it needed completing.

It is my misfortune to have been married to two perfectionist men who won't start a project until they have measured everything three times, lined out all the tools they'd ever need in a million years, and thought about every possible ramification of what they're doing. Me? I subscribe to my former mother-in-law's theory of "Get in, get it done, and if it's not perfect, on a galloping horse, you'll never tell the difference."

Lemonade Man didn't buy the galloping horse theory. Neither did he buy my theory of cutting the wallpaper at corners and starting with a new piece. He wanted to wrap the corners. That's why I immediately gave up the ladder to him, upon finding a corner that was an inch out of square from the top to bottom.

Of course, it didn't help his mood when, in the process of trying to make an untrue corner true, I bopped him in the face with my elbow.

Neither did it help when I forged ahead (he was busy on the ladder, and I was only trying to speed things up) with cutting a second piece of border. It wasn't my fault it didn't match. Why would a manufacturer not start a new border exactly matching the end of the first one? That's how a woman's mind works. A man insists on matching things mathematically. How boring. I interjected some challenge, but the being from another galaxy didn't appreciate that.

As we were both on ladders, with sticky vinyl adhesive all over our arms and realized the wallpaper brush was down on the table and the dogs couldn't retrieve it for us, I made the comment, "I never had this much trouble wallpapering with other women."

Guess who gets to do the dining room all by myself before Christmas? *November 1998*

I've been usurped by 17" wheels and sexy running lights

I always suspected that men preferred hunks of metal to warm flesh. Now it's been confirmed. I couldn't help but be a little jealous recently when Lemonade Man spoke more lovingly of his Ford F-150 than he does of his almost-50 wife.

He calls her "Big Lou," and while he's had this truck for well over a year, he never ceases to admire his possession, asking me to appreciate the sexy running lights on the custom running boards, or to listen to the growl of the engine and the roar of the glass packs he just had to have installed after the neighbor came home with his.

Mechanical gadgets have an allure for the male species that no mere flesh and blood woman can ever compete with. Take the auto-start function on Big Lou. On cold mornings, Lemonade Man just pushes a button from the warmth of the dining room, aims it in Big Lou's direction, and when he's ready for work, the truck is warm and toasty.

"She gets started a lot easier in the mornings than you do," he remarked recently. Could be because all I get is decaf coffee while Big Lou gets an auto-start caress and high-octane fuel.

The really bad thing about the love affair with a truck is that Big Lou has 17" wheels and Lemonade Man is 5'3" and shrinking. His insurance agent still tells the story of this huge truck parking in front of his building and this man getting out of it and then disappearing. It totally dwarfs him. And climbing into it is a feat.

Guess I'll put up with Big Lou because she's great to have for hauling yard waste. The verdict's still out on whether having a big garbage can with running lights is worth diverting and diluting a husband's affections. But if he decides to put one more gadget on the thing, he can start making his bed in it. *March 24, 1999*

Life's no fun unless you get to use the leaf blower

I've spent a good deal of my life waiting on men. Waiting for my turn to kick the football or climb a tree, waiting for one to arrive on time for a date, waiting on one or two to come to the dinner table before the food gets cold.

Another goodly portion of life has been spent watching the males in my life do fun things like tinker with car engines, make things with boards and nails, and run cool machines.

Being a tomboy in a man's world has had its discomforts and disadvantages. I tried to like girl things, honest I did. But after begging as a second grader to be given the responsibility of washing

117

the dishes, I soon found that boring. Ditto house cleaning and babysitting. Let me be outdoors, digging in the dirt, flying a kite, playing cowboys and Indians, or riding a horse, and I was in heaven. That problem plagues me to this day.

While laundry piles up indoors and the kitchen remains cluttered, I make excuses to go to the garden.

While adulthood has allowed me the privilege of pretty much letting the house go while indulging in outdoor chores first, there's still the problem of being a mere spectator in things mostly male. For example, the zero-turn mower is off-limits, as are most of the fancy hand tools. The only part of waxing a car I'm allowed to handle is moving the car forward a few inches to enable the master waxer to more easily do his job.

The excuses used to keep me from these fun things are as follows:

You won't get all the wax off, and it will streak.

You never put the tools back where you found them.

If you want to mow, you'll have to learn to sharpen blades and change the oil too.

You don't clean up your messes.

Last weekend he tired of my whining and let me use the blower to clean off the deck. I'd always wanted to wield that particular power tool (emphasis on the word "power," please, as that's what this is all about). He hollered a set of hurried instructions to me. Something about pressing a bulb three times, putting it on choke, and pulling the cord until it pops. After trying to follow those instructions three times with no luck, Big Guy took the tool out of my hands with some disgust and started it immediately.

All right! I had arrived! I blew myself down the driveway and up the stairs to the deck, blasting everything in my path. The fun lasted all of five minutes. After that, my arms got tired, so I steadied the machine against my leg. Then I noticed the grease stain all over my shorts.

Nobody told me I'd get dirty using power tools.

With the new worn off, I returned the blower to its place of honor on the barn floor, vowing silently not to use it again unless forced to, but calculating that there surely must be a lady version of a blower with the same rpms and a little less heft and grease leakage. Maybe something in a hot pink.

After that, the kitchen and laundry room held a little more appeal, at least until I remembered that I still have not fulfilled a lifelong dream to drive the tractor and use a brush hog. *May 2003*

A new 'do' for the New Year leads directly to the doghouse

We know that we begin aging the minute we're born. But it's the slide into elderhood that some of us have trouble with.

Take Lemonade Man. He'll look at his drooping eyelids, pull them back toward the corners of his eyes and say, "I think I'll get a facelift."

He deals with my aging in the same resistant way. The other day at the dinner table he kept eyeing me with a funny look on his face. Finally, he said, "What's happened to your jaw? It's disappeared!"

Sure enough, it's caving in, melting into the neck below it with no more definition than a turtle's head. We know this happens in our sleep, overnight, because that jawline was there yesterday.

To deal with jawline demise, Santa brought us Andrew Weil's latest book about aging gracefully. He maintains that fighting Mother Nature with plastic surgery and cosmetic potions can be dangerous. We haven't finished the book, but we're expecting it to contain advice about eating right, exercising and breathing correctly, along with accepting gray hairs and sagging chins as badges of courage and wisdom.

Two days before 2005 sang its last hurrah, I decided to get really courageous about this aging stuff and have all my hair cut off. I wanted it to stand up straight in spikes. That would be almost guaranteed to draw the eye away from my non-existent jawline and to my hair, or so I thought.

I tried not to look at the volume of hair that was falling around my shoulders as Kathy Peters whacked it all off, after asking me repeatedly if I was sure this is what I wanted.

"Now, hairspray will be your best friend," she advised as she styled it with her fingers in a method she called "raking." It seems that, in order for spikey hair to stand up, it needs lots of help from the chemical world.

I walked out of the beauty shop feeling ten pounds lighter, with a naked neck, but with smug satisfaction, and walked right into the disapproval of my mate.

"You look like a—man!" was his first comment. That was followed with, "The back of your head looks like a chicken's butt!"

He'd like for me to get my hair styled the way it was when we met 11 years ago. The poor dear doesn't realize the hairstyle doesn't matter when your whole face is suffering from the effects of gravity.

The next day he was watching a national news show and learned that my hairstyle is really "in" for 2006, along with colored highlights. Knowing that he has a wife who's following the latest hair fashion trends provided some comfort and consolation.

I'm afraid there are more men out there who wish they had the courage to be so frank about their own wives' hairstyles and fashions. We visited some relatives last weekend and my cousin had her hair styled in the same spikes. When we related my mate's reaction to my new 'do, my cousin's husband looked at Lemonade Man incredulously and said, "And you're still alive?!" *2006*

Part 5:

Dealing with Disasters by Writing About Them and Laughing at Myself

Backstory

Humor column topics had a way of just falling into my lap. I didn't always go looking for them, but my Type-A personality, my penchant for over-achieving, and for making long to-do lists that set me up for failure often led to situations that many would regard as disasters. To deal with the disasters, I had to let go and laugh at myself. A humor column usually followed, allowing me to gain a new perspective and relieve the tension and stress. I sometimes said that my screwups and disasters allowed my readers to heave a sigh of relief since I had taken their individual screw-up quota for the week.

It wasn't always my own screw-ups that got documented in my humor columns. Lemonade Man was always good for laughter as I shared his disasters—things like pants falling down around knees.

How *not* to put up a ten-foot tree

Next to math, science was my worst subject in school. The algebra teacher called me Charlie Brown, and if it hadn't been for an enormous crush on our biology teacher, I'd never have tried hard and gotten a B in that class.

Last weekend, those teachers would have been proud of my analytical powers and adept trial and error methods. I maneuvered a ten-foot white pine Christmas tree into place, all by myself. It only took four hours.

Fearless Father probably regrets his decision to phone me from Memphis Saturday night where he and The Kid and assorted relatives were staying on their way home from a vacation. I had flown back early to put out the newspaper. The mistake he made was in giving me the go-ahead to decide which tree would grace our house this holiday season and buy it to surprise The Kid when he walked in the door.

Here's the rundown of the great holiday experiment:

Step 1: Go borrow the Old Indian's rusted-out hulk of a pickup that has been parked for a week without receiving his own version of TLC. Try for 15 minutes to start it and keep it going.

Step 2: When told at the local tree farm that there are no white pines available in your normal size range (six to eight feet), opt for a ten-foot one, hurriedly calculating whether the ceilings in the house really are that high and whether Fearless Father will blow a gasket when he hears the price.

Step 3: Use all your considerable weight to drag a huge pine tree out of a pickup and in the front door.

Step 4: When tree gets stuck halfway through the front door, consider taking a picture in case the newspaper needs a good holiday photo as filler. Then figure out that some branches are entangled in the pneumatic door opener and disengage.

Step 5: This step is entitled "How to turn a corner with a ten-foot tree." This probably involves some principle of physics, which course I never took; or maybe geometry, which course I never grasped the fundamentals of. After attacking it from both ends and righting the now-suffering pine, it went through.

Step 6: Go get the saw and test your upper arm strength by making a straight cut across the trunk, like you've seen your husband do every year. Saw off a few lower branches for good measure, only because you've seen that done before too.

Step 7: When it becomes apparent that a tree trunk that measures one foot, five inches in circumference will not go in a stand with a ring measuring one foot, three inches, try your hand at whittling. Then, after your hands are black with pine sap, call Wal-Mart to see if they have any bigger stands. Try not to be insulted when they laugh at you.

Step 8: Call your neighbor for advice. Try not to act hurt when he chuckles and can't offer much except to say you might need a bucket and some sand. (To put my head in maybe?)

Step 9: Head to the Old Indian's place again to steal a bucket and some bricks. Feel a sense of smug self-satisfaction when you see how heavy four bricks in a bucket are. Think to yourself, *There's no* *way this won't work.*

Step 10: Get bucket in place in the corner of the room, ready to receive its tree. Realize, after several trials, that the plastic bucket will break rather than let the tree go in and that two people are definitely needed.

Step 11: Call sweet, kind neighbor, who pushes up the top end while you guide the trunk in place. Thank him profusely and follow his suggestions to scoop up some gravel and sand to help anchor the tree and mentally file a suggestion that it should be wired in place from the ceiling or surrounding windows.

Step 12: Furtively go to the driveway and scoop up gravel, hoping that the neighbors don't think you've lost your marbles and that Fearless Father doesn't miss the rocks. They can be put back in place after Christmas.

Step 13: While filling up the tub with gravel and sand, have the tree fall on your head and come completely out of the bucket. Don't call neighbor again, even if you have to put your back out of place or give yourself a hernia to put the dang thing back in its place.

Step 14: Start looking for wire while you prop the tree in a corner. When there's no wire in the house, go to the store, pine-sap-stained shirt and all, and get some, thanking lucky stars that a grocery store sells picture frame wire and hooks on a Sunday.

Step 15: Climb a ladder and put up two hooks. But don't ever take up more than one hook at a time, so that when you drop one, you'll get lots of exercise going up and down a ladder. When you attach the wire at both ends and around the tree, get it too tight at one end so the tree lists to one side. Then, when you're trying to correct it, the tree will fall, making the whole experience a true trial and error exercise.

Step 16: When you don't think the thing will move, figure out how to water it. When you realize that the low hanging branches will not allow you to tip up anything to pour water from, go get the water hose, turn on the hydrant outside and lie on your stomach to see when the bucket's full. When no water comes out of the hose after three trips to the hydrant, kick out the kinks and cuss. When it does come on and quickly does its job, run like heck to shut it off before the room floods.

That's about all. The only thing I left out was The Kid's comment when he came in and said offhandedly, "That's a Christmas tree." He wanted to know where his surprise was. I'm afraid I might have been a little rude when I pointed to the tree and shouted, "THAT'S YOUR SURPRISE!"

I vow that next year, when The Kid and I are impatiently waiting for Fearless Father to get the tree up so we can decorate it, I will not look at him disgustedly when he cusses and fumes while trying to force a tree trunk into a stand. I will not ask him to turn it around repeatedly, so it hides its bare spots. I might even suggest that we buy an artificial tree. *December 1988*

Give us Tilt-A-Whirls and beds to jump on

Not since last summer's sailboat escapade, where I almost capsized the boat and earned the constant skepticism of my son, have I done anything quite so silly and fun as last weekend.

The excuse was a regional press meeting at the Lake of the Ozarks. It's one of those shirt-sleeves events where everyone brings kids and skips most of the business sessions to go spend money and get over-stimulated on all the lake has to offer.

The fun didn't really start until 9 p.m. when we hit the famous "strip" at Bagnell Dam. That's where a girlfriend and I watched our two sons have their first experience with go-carts. One of them never cracked a smile as he negotiated the tight curves and tried to avoid the side rails. The other looked like one of those bobble-head dolls in the backs of cars as he was jiggled by the G-force exerted by the speed of a lawnmower motor and a bumpy asphalt track. Neither boy could understand why their mothers were laughing so hard, or why we wouldn't ride the silly things ourselves.

We did get in the bumper cars. And while I left at least one vertebra behind, it was so much fun I'd consider having that amusement in my own back yard. It's great for relieving frustrations.

"Remember that time you kicked a window out just because

you were mad at me?" I asked my son, just before ramming his car. "Take that!"

"Well, how about when you spanked me for no reason?" he asked, just before delivering a bone-shattering counterattack. It was better than a boxing match and quite legal.

But the best was yet to come. The tilt-a-whirl! Now that's a ride where two middle-aged women can scream their heads off for a constant 15 minutes and no one will take them to the looney bin. What a tension reliever! What a phlegm clearer! The boys laughed so hard at us they could hardly walk for being doubled over.

The goofy golf game that followed all this idiocy was a letdown and when we returned to the hotel, we were hoping the boys would go to sleep instantly. Instead, they started jumping on the beds. We had just opened our mouths to reprimand them, but decided, "Why not?!" and joined them in childish abandon.

We'll act our age this week, but shoe size was nice for a change.
June 1992

Is there any help for holiday-aholics?

I only wish the Mad Mother could gather up some skepticism about the holidays. It would sure help my bank account. I swore this year that my charge card would not get used for the holidays. I had some money socked away in savings and that was my Christmas budget. Every gift gets written down in a little brown book with the dollar figure to the side. I WILL NOT OVERDO THIS YEAR! But that was before a so-called friend loaned me a set of beautiful holiday decoration books.

If you want to see a creative woman salivate, just give her a glossy, photo-packed book of holiday ideas, and if she's a typical over-achiever, she'll go into overdrive.

There I was Saturday, in front of a cozy fire, with stacks of Christmas cards calling my name. But instead of addressing them, I just sneaked a peek at those books first. The peek turned into total absorption.

Did you know you could decorate your home for the holidays

in any number of themes? There are the quietly elegant, the country, the whimsical, the antique, the 50s, the Victorian...

As I turned the pages, I kept thinking, *Hey, I could do that!* or *That's simple. I've already got the materials I need,* or, *Who would have thought of something like that—greenery in an old flour sifter!* What suckers we can be for putting ourselves into those glossy color photos.

The next morning, like a psychotic Christmas elf, I was outside cutting grapevines and pruning my evergreens. Instead of burning the trimmings, I took them inside my house. That was the inexpensive part.

That afternoon brought a trip to the mega-mall for hobbyists. This is a place where over-achievers go to get over-stimulated and glassy-eyed at aisles of decorative ribbon, plastic vegetables, and paint-by-number tablecloths.

Two hours after entering said hobby mecca, I didn't even wince when the crash register went ka-ching. Didn't even give the bank account balance a second thought as I charged home, dug in The Kid's toy box, rolled up my sleeves, and forgot about unnecessary things like eating and sleeping. Psychologists call this phenomenon "creative flow." In retrospect, I'd call it stupidity.

If something wasn't tied down, it got decorated. It's a good thing The Kid was busy elsewhere or he'd have been sporting a sprig of evergreen and a bow, or would he look better with a few twinkle lights on his head?

The final effect is not quite the same as those glossy photos. But you know, the backs of those books have all kinds of things you can bake for the holidays.

Is there a support group for holiday-aholics? *December 1992*

What happens when old dogs try to learn to snow ski?

For the last decade I've had a yen to try snow skiing. Being a journalist in search of a story gives me a good excuse to visit places and try new things. So, with a few tremors of uncertainty, I headed to Snow Creek near Weston last week to write a story about a sport that is apparently as captivating and addictive as golf.

The interview with resort manager David Grenier went smoothly. But smoothness ended the minute I walked out of his office.

The girl at the ticket window looked at me expectantly as I stammered, "I guess I want to learn to ski." She handed me a form to fill out indicating the skill level I had attained in the sport, then a ticket that reminded me of those things you don't want to pull off a mattress for fear of being arrested, and finally, a metal clip that looked like a shower curtain ring.

From there, I followed the hundreds of other beginners who were taking advantage of a Learn to Ski Free Day at Snow Creek. Form filled out indicating a skill level of "zilch," I showed up at the ski boot counter and accepted a pair of heavy footwear, headed to the bathroom, and locked myself in the handicapped stall to put on ski bibs and figure out how to install feet in ski boots.

The first shock came from trying to walk in lead weights that don't bend. Had to trade in the first pair, since they were too roomy. That required producing the slip of paper that I'd somehow lost in the frenzy of trying to reopen an uncooperative pay locker. Nothing is ever uncomplicated when you're scared speechless.

Finally made it to the ski counter, where a kindly senior citizen clerk patiently explained the mechanics of putting boots into skis and of unhooking them when you get into trouble. Poles selected, I set out the door to conquer the world—or at least a few feet of snowy slope. It conquered me instead. Three minutes after skis were attached to boots, I was on the ground eating snow.

The endlessly-patient instructors at Snow Creek were positioned at ten stations to teach us the fundamentals. There were so many of us that we stood in line 20 minutes just waiting to get to the first lesson. That gave me time to get used to the feel of the boots and relax a little.

The first station was dedicated to hopping up and down in skis to warm up and learning safety rules. I was not the only skeptic who wondered how in the world you ski in control when you have no idea how to affect the direction of the slippery sticks underneath you.

From there, we learned the jargon and motions of a foreign sport—things like the bullfighter's stance, wedging (all I can remember is "pizza," which is what they kept shouting at us to make us remember how to position our skis), climbing up hills sideways, traversing, and how to get up from a fall. One of the instructors reminded me of a high school football coach and driver's ed instructor I had. I couldn't ever do anything right at his station because of an irrational feeling of intimidation and stupidity.

During the course of the next four exhausting hours, I lost my hat four times, fell down 20, developed painful blisters on the insides of my feet, got snow down my pants, knocked over about four other people, and wore out the palms of a pair of new gloves trying to grab onto the icy rope tow. At one point I almost started to bawl, "I can't do this," and, "I give up." That was after I reached for a Kleenex and discovered my ski jacket was on wrong side out and I couldn't remember how it got that way.

About dusk, I looked at the little munchkins going down the slope like speed demons with no ski poles and then looked at myself, trying to simply locomote on a straightaway to the rope tow line and realized I'd had enough. For perhaps the first time in my life, I knew the reality of sheer physical exhaustion. I sat in the car for a full five minutes trying to regain control of my weak limbs, shivering uncontrollably in wet clothes, and realizing why ski country is populated with hot tubs and people lots younger and more athletic than me. The car made it to the first Long John Silver's, where a combination platter disappeared in five minutes flat.

I made it home in time to start feeling the twinges of whole-body soreness. That night I couldn't sleep. Like a dog who twitches in his sleep, dreaming of chasing rabbits, my leg muscles were still trying to do the right turns and wedges and get in the bullfighter's stance to come into position with skis.

You'd think I'd never want to set foot on a ski slope again, right? Wrong! I'll go back the first chance I get. No stupid snowbank is gonna get the best of me. I wear my first lift ticket on my ski jacket as a badge of honor. And I recall how my mother learned to water ski after age 40. She downed a beer first. So, I'll be looking for an old bottle of peppermint schnapps to add to a thermos of hot chocolate before hitting the slopes the next time. *January 1993*

Danger: Middle-aged wild women on the loose; last seen shoe shopping

Everybody needs a friend they can get in trouble with. By long-delayed pre-arrangement, I met one of them at a city mega mall Saturday.

We celebrated my birthday with a pig-out at a restaurant, showing off photos of our families and catching up on each other's news. She picked up the tab, which was a darn sight better than my actual birthday dinner the night before when I paid to take my son to see a movie I didn't want to see, then rushed him home from a restaurant after he barfed up the clam chowder.

With eating out of the way, Chris and I settled in for some serious shopping. She'd been looking for a billfold for three months and I needed some school clothes for The Kid. The object here was not the purchasing (she still didn't buy a billfold) but the camaraderie and the cutting up. When the day ended, we agreed to maybe go into training before we met again and perhaps cash in a CD so the fun could be better financed.

The highlight of the day was stumbling into a *ginormous* store that was holding a grand opening. This former grocery store was now filled to the gills with brand-name discount shoes. The store clerks were dressed in tuxedos and a disc jockey interspersed blue light specials every ten minutes with too-loud rock music. The crowds were wild.

When we finally got to a breathing space right past the front door, elbowing frantic shoppers aside along the way, we grabbed each other and said simultaneously and tearfully, "Don't leave me again!" We stopped short of buying one of those kiddie leashes and got serious about our respective shoe fetishes.

At one point I made the mistake of following the crowds

pushing to a special on some Candies flats for $7 a pair. The next fifteen minutes were spent trying to reconnect with Chris, walking down every center aisle and looking both ways. Finally, I heard the disc jockey announce much too loudly, "Will Anne please meet Chris at the front of the store? She's lost and you're now embarrassed."

I was so glad I was far from home and didn't know a soul in that store. I was also glad it was Chris driving and not me when she pulled out of the parking spot and clipped the next car.

We concluded we were bad influences on each other, spending way too much money and getting into too much trouble (she wasn't going to tell her husband about the car). Still, we're already making plans to meet again soon for another marathon excursion. You might want to watch for us and park real far away. *September 1, 1993*

Can camping be as much fun as the contemplation?

Lemonade Man's winter project has been the intense study of the hobby of camping. Instead of looking at seed catalogs, we've been looking at tent campers, going to RV shows, and making lists of camping supplies. This from a man who has never been camping in his life. He has no idea what he's in for.

As a veteran of tent camping, I tried to tell him that setting up camp is not a thing guaranteed to improve marriages, that tent poles and canvas have a way of sparking sharp words. And he doesn't quite understand that in order to go camping you practically have to cart along your entire household.

She persists. He falls asleep with pop-up camper floor plans on his face, and our primary topics of discussion lately have been whether we should look for a model with a cassette toilet and shower separate from each other or in the same compartment, and whether to buy Corelle for camping or try to locate some old Melmac.

For those of you who haven't been to an RV show lately, the once modest pop-up has grown up. The interiors have moved from your basic brown plaids to Southwestern motifs complete with fancy curtain valances, air conditioners, furnaces, refrigerators, and bathrooms. You can even buy a motorized crank so the thing pops up in eight minutes. Some models have a storage compartment in front to hold your fishing supplies, lawn chairs, etc. and a screen room to keep the mosquitos away.

Lemonade Man's main concern, aside from having a toilet separate from the shower so he doesn't have to step in cold water at 3 a.m. after someone has showered in the evening, is snakes. He wants something that's guaranteed to be snake-tight. This city boy has an abhorrence for snakes that makes him go for the shotgun if he encounters a little garter in the garden. When he does buy a camper, you can bet it will be one that is Velcroed so tightly that not even an ant could get inside.

Then we have the fear of break-ins. The man who has had a brand-new vehicle stolen and stripped and left for dead on Quindaro in Kansas City thinks a tent camper needs a motion sensor and alarm system. He has visions of knives splitting the canvas and thieves stealing our precious Melmac.

I've tried to tell him that the people who go camping are good folks not prone to stealing. In fact, the only thieves we ever ran into while camping as youngsters were skunks and raccoons, who sifted through the garbage.

We have a potentially dangerous situation here. But the months of study will not be for naught. The camper will probably come rolling into the driveway someday soon, followed by weeks of stocking it and figuring out all the mechanical idiosyncrasies. Then comes tough decisions.

Do we take the dogs? Will they stay inside without chewing cushions while we go have fun. Do we take The Kid and a friend? Do we buy matching bedspreads? Where do we go for our maiden voyage? Who do we know that lives nearby and will let us camp by their farm pond and go fishing, so that when we forget something, we can unhook the truck and go back to town after it?

Of course, the primary benefit to all these agonizing decisions is that we're a little closer to spring and our time this winter has been spent thinking about something that could end up being enjoyable.

Give me a starry summer sky, a campfire and a marshmallow stick, and a good book to relax with, and I'll be happy, even in a tent. Give Lemonade Man a snake-free environment and a lake full of fish and breakfast cooked outdoors and he'll be content. *February 1998*

Look out fellow campers, here we come!

Now I remember why I like camping so much. Last weekend's summer-like weather allowed us to open our new pop-up and "test drive" it right in our own backyard.

There's just something incomparable about having only a thin mesh screen and a bit of canvas separating you from the great outdoors, sleeping under the stars, and wondering whether that thing crawling on your skin is a bug that bites.

Two weekends ago, we almost took the little home on wheels back to the dealer.

It was time to mow under the camper, so it had to be moved. It happened to be pretty soft underfoot, making the operation a supreme challenge. When the wheel jack on the trailer hitch kept sinking deeper in the mud, Mad Mother gets the brilliant idea to go after the hydraulic jack. The jack, placed on top of a 4x4, gave us the leverage to raise the front of the camper enough to clear the ball hitch on the truck. As Lemonade Man jumped in the cab of the Ford to back 'er up, he warned me not to move that jack. But he didn't get it lined up perfectly. It was an inch too far to the west. I decided it wouldn't hurt to move it just a teensy bit. The jack promptly fell out from under the hitch and the trailer teetered precariously—all 2,000 pounds of it. I thought I was going to see a grown man cry.

He started over, with me far removed from the scene. I came back in time to see Lemonade Man make three attempts at re-positioning the trailer on a stack of 4x4s for leveling, glaring at me all the while as if it was my fault he couldn't hit the broad side of a narrow board.

We got through that scene without a divorce. The true test will be this weekend when we take the camper out to a real campground.

In the meantime, we had a pretty good dry run last weekend.

Lemonade Man spent Saturday reading his owner's manual, hooking up drain hoses, putting chemicals in the toilet, flushing the water tank, and generally puttering. I was inside, making lists, getting out the coffee pot, and trying to decide where to put things for cooking and cleaning up and for living temporarily in a ten-foot box on wheels.

We ate supper inside that box, with the June bugs buzzing to join the party. We sprawled on the couch to watch a movie on the portable TV, before retiring to our Martha Stewart-decorated bunks.

The next morning, Lemonade Man tried out the shower and I fixed hash browns, bacon, and eggs—things that always taste better cooked and eaten outdoors.

The good feelings of being 20 feet away from the house but not inside to face the clutter persisted through the day. I actually got to start reading a good book. We ate two more meals in the camper and slept under the stars again, even though it was a school night for The Kid.

There was only minor cussing and glaring going on as we folded away the camper in last night's heat and humidity. It was ready to go to a real campground.

Lemonade Man is re-reading the camper manual, consulting the camping veterans in the neighborhood, and dreading his first attempt at backing into a real campsite. Mad Mother is making lists, planning a baking spree, and packing a novel, sunscreen, bug repellent, and some high hopes for more rest and relaxation. This will be a real test of whether two overweight, middle-aged, out-of-shape people have any business with a camper, and whether a teen-aged boy will be bored stiff with our attempts at having fun. *May 1998*

Terror in the dark at Ruidoso, New Mexico

It had been three years since Lemonade Man and Mad Mother had a real, honest-to-goodness vacation. But we did the normal vacation stress routine—doing two weeks' work in one, arranging for someone to keep our plants and animals alive in our absence, etc., as we prepared to head to Ruidoso, New Mexico for a week.

We had no idea what awaited us. Everyone raised their eyebrows when they heard New Mexico. "You're leaving hot for hotter?!" they asked incredulously.

"Oh well, at least it'll be a dry hot," we always replied, consoling ourselves with the fact that this was the only condo timeshare available in the whole country for the week we could go.

As we traveled through the familiar Kansas feedlot territory and spent the night in Tucumcari (just like the billboards advised), the land opened up into our stereotype of New Mexico. We saw mesquite and scrub pines in a vista broken only by occasional mesas. I read and The Kid napped with his headphones on in the back seat. But gradually the landscape changed. We were climbing.

Ruidoso sits in the middle of a saddle of mountains, with the highest, Sierra Blanca, at 7,200 feet. That makes the weather in this resort town absolutely optimal. While the rest of you were sweltering back home, we were enjoying evening temps of 50s and 60s and daytimes in the 80s. When we did venture out for day trips to Carlsbad Caverns and White Sands, the heat was enough to practically mummify us on the spot. But we quickly beat a retreat to our mountain hideaway and used the condo kitchen to fix meals and save money. It was that money-saving that got me into trouble.

Lemonade Man requested a mess of his famous country-style barbecue ribs, so he parboiled the meat and told The Kid and I to throw the drippings out the back window, since to throw it out the front door would have made us look like the Missouri Clampitts.

In the wee hours of the night, it occurred to me that throwing meat drippings outside a bedroom window in bear country may not have been the smartest move. Suddenly, I heard a noise like an animal licking or slurping. At 3 a.m., the worst time for night terrors, as your mind can kick into overdrive. I did re-runs in my head of all the bear mauling stories I'd ever seen on the Discovery Channel and nearly made myself sick. I fumbled for my glasses and tiptoed to the window. Nothing furry moved, and it was raining, so maybe the noise was just water dripping from leaves. I sighed with relief and went back to bed, but not without waking Lemonade Man, who had to hear the night terror story. He was absolutely no comfort. Instead, just as I finally dozed off to sleep, I felt something licking my face and heard growling.

You know, men are really sick human beings.

The next day we asked a few shopkeepers about bears. They said they were very common in the area and that you should never leave garbage or meat scraps anywhere near the house at night. They also told us the story of the Texan whose son came into their vacation home in Ruidoso to say there was a bear outside. The tough Texan got his gun out and shot the beast that was so tame he actually waved at tourists. The locals ran the Texan out of town and erected a statue to memorialize the beast they all called the Cinnamon Bear.

Apparently, New Mexicans are protective and proud of their bears, while this Missourian is touchy about husbands who pretend to be bears at 3:30 a.m. *August 1999*

Cardinal rules for campers: A timely primer

You may recall from this column a few years ago, our first round at using our tent camper was a Memorial Day trip to an area campground where our main activity was keeping a cloudburst from spoiling every bit of fun. That was the last time we used the toy—until last weekend.

We headed out Friday morning, bound for Finger Lakes State Park to meet Motorcycle Mama and Pistol Pete. We had picked the location because it was only 15 minutes from their home in Columbia and it had a group of lakes bound to be full of fish.

We learned more about camping. Here's a primer for the uninitiated:

•A camp dedicated to people with ATVs is not exactly quiet. Nor is it clean, since the people who favor this sport like to slosh through the biggest puddles they can find, leaving a trail of muddy clothes and tracks on the pavement.

•A camp full of muddy people requires the frequent use of shower facilities, leading to the depletion of sources of hot water, leading in turn to women screaming in agony when they step under a cold stream of water at 10 p.m.

•A man determined to fish in 98-degree weather at 3 p.m., mainly because he has purchased minnows, is bound for some grief. In this case, Lemonade Man decided not to follow the expedition, and instead, chose a nap in the air-conditioned camper, while the remainder of the troops followed the oldest member (the one concerned about the health of the minnows).

With sweat dripping down our backs, we launched the fishing boat and headed out to sea (actually, a quarry pit converted to a fishing lake). Halfway to a shady spot, Pistol Pete remembers his minnows are sweltering in the back of the pickup. He drops us off on the opposite shore and tries to head back for the bait, but a wind comes up and the trolling motor doesn't want to push him back to the boat launch.

Meanwhile, back at the steep bank where the women wait with poles, tackle, and a jug of water, we notice some suspicious looking leaves—was it poison oak or ivy? Then there were the little critters crawling on us that cause Rocky Mountain Spotted Fever, Tularemia, and Lyme Disease.

We hailed the frustrated boat pilot, jumped back aboard, and Motorcycle Mama began rowing against a brisk wind, managing to lose the shade umbrella in the lake. After retrieving the errant minnows, we settled in the shade. I was the only one to catch anything other than a tick and sunburn.

•When a pop-up camper with an air conditioner sits without use for two years, critters find their way into the unit. Said discovery made at 2 a.m. when the cool stopped being cool. It was still 85 degrees at that time of the morning, so we sweltered through the night until restarting the unit in the morning and discovering it was filled with wasp nest debris.

•When it rains two inches in two hours and you're encased in a canvas contraption, there's no way to keep out dampness, especially noticeable on pillows at bedtime.

•When someone in your party has lost his good hearing aid and you're all watching a movie on your little camping TV and have to turn it up all the way, you get a knock on your camper door from the friendly park ranger. At which point you invite him in for a beer, knowing he's not allowed to accept, but thinking it might help smooth the situation a bit.

•The main attractions in camping are the relaxation, the stress reduction, and the food. For two days we forgot about phones, deadlines, and the heartburn that occurs during the workweek. We are now veterans, ready for another foray into the wilderness that includes chemical toilets, a hot shower, TV, and comfortable bunk.

Except that Lemonade Man is planning to run a for-sale ad real soon. He would prefer a Super 8. It's less work. *June 2000*

The last days of summer beckon us to pitch a tent on the driveway

It was one of those weekends where you feel compelled to cram every last summer activity into 48 hours, knowing that the cold days are coming soon.

Friday night we rushed through supper so we could take a drive to Dairy Queen with the top down on the Miata for summer's last ice cream cone. There were a few priceless moments of daylight left upon our return, so we decided to put up the tent that came with Lemonade Man's new pickup.

It's one of those tents you see in the slick vehicle brochures—one that was supposed to fit in the bed of the truck. By the time I read the assembly instructions, written by non-English speaking persons and with no accompanying diagrams or photos, it was dark, and the mosquitoes decided to have us for dessert. Two trips to the house later, we had the cute little contraption put together. Then, nothing would do but go inside to get the air mattress, pump it up, and see what it would feel like to look at the stars from the back of a pickup, behind the safety of mosquito-net windows. But the fun stopped there, because we had to go back in and finish canning the last of the garden tomatoes.

Saturday was frittered away in a day trip and an evening steak dinner in the city. Sunday was likewise wasted with Lemonade Man watching the Chief's game on a porch swing outdoors, after he rigged up a cable that snaked all the way into his downstairs office and out to the patio. I read a book in the hammock, and we had company over for a laid-back dinner.

But Sunday night, we felt compelled to try the truck camping thing. We had scoped out a nice spot on the crest of a hill overlooking the pond. We brushed our teeth, got on our jammies, and climbed in the truck. Halfway there, Lemonade Man, ever the city boy, said, "Why don't we just park it in the driveway so we won't get chiggers all over our feet when we get out?"

I reluctantly agreed. Instead of looking out over the pond, we'd have to settle for just the moon and Mars and blacktop. I had already foolishly agreed to let him take a big claw hammer with us as a weapon to defend ourselves in case we were confronted with who-knows-what on the driveway.

After the major feat of two over-50 people climbing into the bed of a 4x4 truck was accomplished, we settled in comfortably and drew the covers up to our noses. Lemonade Man insisted on hearing some tent camping stories from my childhood days of tent camping. After the stories ended (without including the ghost stores we told in those days) silence descended, except for the chirping of crickets and the sound of traffic on the interstate a mile away.

Soon I felt a poke in my ribs and a whispered, "What was that sound?"

I told him it was probably a raccoon, and to go to sleep. He really did try, but when I was about to doze off, he says, "Did they ever catch that guy that escaped from the Pattonsburg jail?"

That did it. He got into the cab of the truck and I zipped up the tent. We drove back to the house and went upstairs to our own comfortable bed, behind a securely-locked door.

So much for pickup bed camping. Maybe, if no more prisoners escape, and if all the mosquitoes and chiggers in North Missouri are somehow eradicated, we'll give pickup bed camping another try.

September 2003

The Ides of April, when birds fly sideways and hambones burn

If you're a student of astrology, you probably know that the alignment of the earth, moon, and sun right now is cause for temporary concern. Each spring this happens, and it's not good. It's the time of year when ponds turn over and birds fly sideways. This must be the origin of the old insult, "If you put his brain in a bluejay it would fly sideways."

During this treacherous time, we're to be especially careful to avoid accidents. We know this firsthand.

Sunday saw yours truly head to the office for some catchup work. As I pulled out of the driveway, I asked Lemonade Man for his cellphone (don't like to leave home without it and didn't want to go all the way back in the house for mine). He was getting ready for some heavy-duty lawn mower maintenance, but he had also put a pot of navy beans on the stove with an Easter hambone.

About 3 p.m. I got a call at the office from an employee who was on the notification list for our alarm company. Our smoke alarm was going off at the house and the alarm company couldn't reach anyone on our landline phone or on cellphones. I had forgotten to turn on the borrowed one. So, they had dispatched the fire department.

Meanwhile, back at the ranch, Lemonade Man was busy filling different gas containers with mixes for the weed whacker and mower, oblivious to the hambone and beans. That is, until the fire chief pulled up to the barn with a screech, lights flashing. Before the two pumper trucks arrived, my dear husband thought something had happened to me on the highway and nearly went into cardiac arrest.

But heart attack or not, he was going into that house to rescue the dogs and family photos. He charged ahead of firemen, as fast as his short legs would allow, and found the upstairs engulfed in smoke.

Remember that 45 mph wind that blew on Sunday? It helped clear the smoke when windows and doors were opened for three hours. As a paramedic took Lemonade Man's blood pressure and advised him to go to the hospital if it didn't calm down, the fire chief said another 15 minutes would have meant an insurance claim for smoke damage. We lucked out.

Since our dinner burned, we had supper out. Halfway through our tortilla chips, a speeding waitress dropped a tray of glasses and steak sauce, splattering customers with glass and liquids. After the mess was mopped up and a few other waitresses nearly broke their necks on the oil slick left behind, we warned everyone within earshot about the ill-fated alignment of the moon, earth, and sun so they could be on guard against bluejays flying sideways and other astrological manifestations.

Then last night at a meeting in Breckenridge, B. J. Gray was telling someone about the perfect Easter hambone she had put on the stove Sunday with some beans. Someone came to pick her up to go get her riding lawnmower. Well, you know the rest of the story. Except hers didn't involve the arrival of two pumper trucks and an ambulance.

I don't think this alignment will last past tonight. Then we can all start worrying about tornado season. *April 2004*

Blame it on the lima beans

At our house, a casual suggestion of a need usually produces prompt results. Lemonade Man can't stand procrastination, so when he heard me mention last weekend that the lima beans I planted needed something to vine on, he went into action.

Picture the city boy/pretend weekend farmer at Orscheln's, surrounded by overall-clad non-imposters. Imagine the snorts of derision he got when he told the clerk he wanted a three-foot section of hog or cattle panel. "They don't come that way," he was told with a smirk.

When I got home from a city council meeting last night, the back end of the pickup was loaded with a bent cattle panel that would have beheaded a tall man if somebody had opened the tailgate without being poised for flight.

This morning, before he even had his first cup of coffee, Lemonade Man was determined to deal with that cattle panel, with a little help from his wife.

"Now I'm gonna back up straight to the garden," he warned me as he climbed into the pickup. Okay. Only problem was, the cattle panel struck up five feet above the cab and the tree on the road to the garden hung down lower. As the cattle panel began to look like latticework oak, I was in front of the truck yelling and gesticulating to the confused driver, who was as highly offended at my yelling as I get when he does the same thing. But he stopped and drove forward, then back again, only to impale the cattle panel anew on the tree branches.

"Those branches were too low anyway," he rationalized, after checking his favorite vehicle for oakwood scratches and taking a few limbs to the brush pile.

We unloaded the cattle panel and three metal fence stakes to hold it upright, walking on the wire to get the overnight kink out of it. Price tag to stake half a row of lima beans: $35. Kodak moment in the continuing saga of city slickers trying to get by in the country: priceless.

My margin of superiority (due to spending the first four years of my life on a farm of 20 acres) evaporated as I was helping him load some chemical tanks in the back of the truck for a trip to the city to spray his stepmom's yard for fleas and ticks. I put the wrong foot in the step of the tailgate. The treads of my sneaker caught in the rung of the funky little ladder and over I went, onto the asphalt, like the Sta-Puff marshmallow woman. It was Lemonade Man's turn to laugh, paybacks for last week's tango with the garden hose.

The day has deteriorated even more since the great fall. Picture coleslaw decorating the kitchen floor. Actually, it goes well with the Berber carpet. You can't even see the pieces that didn't get picked up.

We can blame it all on the lima beans. All I know is, they'd better cooperate and climb up that cattle panel. *July 2004*

Get plenty of rest before going fishing

Dogs and thunderstorms don't make good bedfellows.

For the past two nights our best friends have given us the option of putting up with toenail-scarred door frames or them in bed with us. I don't know who told me in my childhood that thunder was God unloading his wagon of potatoes in heaven, but that metaphor is totally useless with four-legged children, as is every attempt to soothe them in the midst of a lightning show and thunder soundtrack.

One of the beasts is so frightened she gets under the covers and scooches down to the foot of the bed, preferring possible suffocation and the smell of toes to subjecting herself to death by thunder.

Yesterday, with weather-related arthritis and no sleep setting the pattern for his day, Lemonade Man made the mistake of trying to improve his mood by going fishing after work.

You should see what happens when an otherwise avid and skilled fisherman has a bad day behind a rod and reel. His first mistake was in not applying insect repellent. The second was putting off restringing of reels. By putting off, we're talking in the past 15 years. As we learned last night, monofilament does get as old and brittle as people do.

While Lemonade Man was cussing an open-bale reel that was malfunctioning, my third cast into the old farm pond resulted in a lost jig. It was all downhill from there.

We battled skinny, dried-out worms, broken line after broken line, malfunctioning floats, hooks that disappeared right after they'd been attached to leaders, and bait that slithered through the cracks in the dock. A trip back to the house to get a better rod and reel was wasted when he spent his entire time fixing my broken lines and swatting the bugs that landed on his insecticide-free arms.

In an episode that would make for good slapstick, this going-on-60 man actually got his hook caught under the dock just before I lost my line and float to a good-sized bass. We finally sat on the dock and watched catfish roll and bass jump, after catching two nice size largemouths, and throwing them back in when they broke the lines.

When we got back to the house, the man with no sleep pulled every single one of his rods off the garage wall, carted them upstairs, and started dismantling them. Nothing like a bad day at the dock, after a night of severe thunderstorms, to make you stop procrastinating.

Now the challenge is that the revamped fishing equipment suddenly needs a bigger tackle box. And it wouldn't hurt to have a reel re-winder. Then, while he's at it, it's time for some new jigs.

I wonder if homeowner's insurance covers new fishing equipment purchases caused by thunder and lightning? *August 2004*

Girl Scout cookies and politics in the same box?

We had a roundtable discussion at work this afternoon over a slice of warm banana bread. Everyone had an opinion about what I should write about in my column this week. The topics ranged from school shootings to the Terri Schiavo case and also included sex and Girl Scout cookies.

My strongest feelings revolve around the last topic. Whoever invented the very first sale of Girl Scout cookies was a marketing genius. He/she took advantage of perfect timing to instill in us an automatic sensing device that begins in early March to perk up with the thought, *Isn't it time for my cookies to come in?*

This being the season of church and self-induced guilt called Lent, the promise of the decadence of a Thin Mint is almost enough to cause you to sin and fall back in it—the cookie I mean—and no sacrilege intended.

One of our employees had a minor tiff with her husband this week. He wanted to know what she'd done with the extra box of cookies he knew they had purchased this year. She admitted she had stashed it in the freezer, saving it for when their college daughter came home for spring break. He grudgingly admitted that was acceptable, but he'll probably try to cajole a few out of that box too.

Much to my chagrin, I learned during our roundtable discussion that some idiot has sternly admonished the Girl Scouts for the trans fats in their fund-raising products. Next thing we know, the poor girls will be sued for making people fat. Or someone will accuse them of putting an aphrodisiac in their Animal Treasures (that chocolate coating on the back of those shortbreads is to die for!).

Soon we'll have a congressional inquiry into the corruption inherent in putting cute little girls on the streets peddling boxes of decadent delights that are not good for us.

I can't form a coherent opinion on the Terry Schiavo case. It's too complex and emotional Too fraught with politics and hints of spousal abuse—along with the futility of someone who is in a "persistent vegetative state."

And while the latest school shooting is cause for alarm and consternation, as Americans we again shy away from the complex social genesis of the story. We become numb and dumb about it, just like we become jaded about the threat of another terrorist attack.

But eat all the Girl Scout cookies in the box and we've got a knock-down, drag-out on our hands—a veritable local riot.

This is not just an isolated phenomenon. My sister-in-law just reminded me that her sister and partner-in-cookie-crimes has a whole drawer full of Girl Scout cookies, just waiting for the end of Lent. I'm invited to the orgy, but only if I eat the Lemon Cremes and save the Thin Mints for them. *March 2005*

Beware: Binge cooking hazardous to health and hands

My name is Anne and I'm a binge cook.

During a normal week I don't attempt anything more complicated or creative than goulash. But give me a three-day holiday weekend and I totally lose control in the kitchen.

Usually, this time of year my cooking binges are induced by a surfeit of zucchini and tomatoes. Saturday was spent at the controls of a food processor, grating the big yellow zucs we grew this year. With the aid of chopping blades and a rubber spatula, the oven was soon full of two loaves of zucchini bread. But that was only after a loaf of banana bread had been fashioned from the black bananas that had been hanging on a hook in the kitchen for a few days. And only after I'd cleaned out the pantry and found a box of bread mix and filled up the breadmaker with those ingredients. I was on an uncontrollable roll!

The main portion of grated zucchini went into a big bowl, to be combined with peppers, onion, and salt to soak overnight for relish. The day ended with the remnant of good kitchen smells filling the air. I went to bed tired but terribly pleased with myself.

The next day after church found me once again indulging in cooking addiction. The zucchini relish was beginning to simmer on the stove, and I was washing jars in the sink so they could be sterilized for canning the relish. In the industrious frenzy aided by two cups of caffeine and little breakfast that morning, I had my hand inside a pint jar when there came an unfamiliar tug of skin on the outside of my right hand. Taking hand out of jar I noticed from an objective distance, "Oh, that's my hand sliced open a few inches deep."

A dish towel formed a temporary blood-stopper as I walked up the hill to the barn where Lemonade Man was indulging in his own binge of car washing and debugging. "Um, I think I need to go to the emergency room," I told him calmly.

I now sport four stitches, but by golly, there are seven jars of the most expensive relish in the world now lining my kitchen counter. I'm thinking of labeling it "Emergency Room Relish." Lemonade Man is busy figuring what it cost the family to can it, not counting my time. He's good at that.

Meanwhile, I'm starting to get the urge to sew something. Let's see if I can put a sewing machine needle through my finger.
September 2005

Shake 'n' Burn, and I helped!

Some television commercials stick with you for decades. Remember the one with the kid proudly showing how he could help Mom fry chicken for Sunday dinner with Shake 'n' Bake coating mix? In an unmistakable Midwestern twang, the child said excitedly, "Look! Shake 'n' Bake! And I helped!"

That jingle came to mind when I got home one night last week to a husband who was trying to be helpful by starting supper. When I walked in the house, something smelled a little off. My sensitive culinary nose detected overdone onion and burned grease. I came upstairs to a mate who was more than a little sheepish. He immediately began stammering excuses about "just trying to help."

I noticed every window in the house was open and the air conditioner was still running. "Uh oh! Did we have a little fire, scarecrow?" I asked.

"Just a little smoke," came the reply. Also, a little bitty call from the alarm company and another from the fire department. They all got to hear about Chicken Gone Wrong.

He now knows that you can't take four chicken wings and put them into a one-egg skillet filled with olive oil and expect anything but disaster, especially on a ceramic stovetop.

Picture man cleaning cook top with razor blade for an hour, digging frantically at crystallized oil after greeting me with the words, "I think I just ruined your new stove."

The stove still works. It had a large pressure cooker used on the same burner over the weekend. And when we ran into a friend over the weekend who got to hear the shake and burn episode, he felt sheepish all over again at seeing her raised eyebrows and hearing, "Don't you know you're not supposed to deep fry anything with olive oil?"

He would have felt bad until she told him that the same day he was burning chicken wings, she put a TV dinner in the microwave and hit an extra zero in the timing, so that four minutes became 40. She wondered why her little dog kept running back and forth to the kitchen while she was trying to watch the news until she saw what barbecue riblets look and feel like when they're permanently bonded to a plastic tray.

So, now that a few cooking disasters are history, we can concentrate on really important matters … like chigger bites and the lack of ripe tomatoes in the land. *2009*

Will a kitchen divided endure a food fight?

For the past few years, I've been trying to consume a healthier diet. That involves shying away from bad trans fats, high fructose corn syrup, preservatives, and foods with high sugar content. In the past few months, I even gave up coffee and other caffeinated beverages, since my self-education allowed me to visualize the calcium leaching out of my bones from the stimulant. I'm now at the point of reading nutrition labels on foods and if there are too many items I can't pronounce, they don't get put in the shopping cart.

My initiation into healthy food took a step forward in the past few weeks with my interviews of organic farmers and livestock producers who grass feed their animals. One of those producers graciously sent me home with a package of organic pork chops and organic beef steaks.

Lemonade Man will acknowledge the benefits of healthy eating. After all, he's the one with diabetes in the family. I just suffer from other modern maladies that stem from poor nutrition. But last week I put the organic pork chops on the grill for supper. The first thing we noticed was a pink blush to the meat that differs greatly from the chops of mass producers. In fact, it reminded us of the pork chops our grandparents and parents used to fix. The fat is even a slightly different color.

I found the organic pork totally delicious. It had a different flavor, but a decidedly good taste. City boy, on the other hand, sniffed the meat, declared it had a "whang" and swore he tasted chickweed and fescue, and pushed his plate away. I just took the other chops to work, and a fellow health food nut relished them as much as I did.

Now we're battling over brown eggs. Ever since Lemonade Man had a brown egg that had a residue of straw from the nest, and since the day he encountered a blood spot in a yolk, he's been determined not to have a healthy egg enter his mouth. We now have two egg cartons in our refrigerator. When I fix two Eggland's Best eggs for him, I show him how my brown egg yolk stands up tall and proud, while his look pale and flat. He won't listen to the fact that my pasture-raised, free-range chicken eggs have more Omega 3s than his and that mine came off the farm two days ago and his could be as far away from the hens as seven months.

The only point he concedes in this food fight is the purchase of free-range chickens, as he's quite suspicious of the huge chicken breasts that come frozen in big bags, sure he's eating hormones.

Our kitchen promises to become a segregated one—with one side for grassfed and the other for mass-produced. He tells me, "What difference does it make? I'm going to die of something anyway. Might as well enjoy my food while I'm getting ready to buy the farm."

He will not be joining me if I ever go on a cooking tour of France. Currently I'm trying to figure out if he'll let me convert part of the barn to a chicken coop and if the garden shed can be converted to a smokehouse. I will try to issue a progress report from the front lines when the battle smoke clears. *August 2010*

Having a meltdown while burning sugar

All I wanted to do last week was to re-create the birthday cake my mom made for my ninth birthday anniversary. It was the best cake I'd ever put in my mouth. She called it a Martha Washington cake.

A diligent Google search finally turned up what sounded like the recipe she must have used. An upcoming employee birthday celebration gave me the excuse I needed to turn back the clock to a delicious day.

I read the recipe several times and made a trip to the store to complete the checklist of ingredients. The cake wasn't much of a worry. It was the icing that stumped me. I remember it being a caramel confection that perfectly complemented the rich, baked-from-scratch cake. Burnt-sugar icing rang a bell.

Several cookbooks later, I zeroed in on Betty Crocker as the one with the answer.

My first mistake was starting this baking project at the end of a workweek, at the end of a long day, when all I wanted to do was take a nap on the couch and be entertained by *American Idol* on TV.

The second mistake was in putting my trust in a programmable microwave. Don't believe a machine that tells you it can soften butter with one button. Two sticks of butter running all over the microwave tray is not a pretty sight.

The third mistake was in the use of cake flour, something I've never bought in my life, but decided a special cake must take special flour.

The fourth mistake was using two 9-inch cake pans and an 8-inch pan to come up with a three-layer cake. The whole thing was actually doomed from that point onward.

The fifth mistake was in thinking that to burn sugar to make burnt sugar icing, raw sugar would work just as well as refined white and would be healthier to boot. Ha! Guess how bad a beautiful, perfectly-seasoned iron skillet can look when raw sugar caramelizes along the edges in what appears to be permanent concrete?

The sixth mistake was in taking a cup full of hot, burned sugar syrup with a spoon to Lemonade Man to taste. His expert tastebuds always come to the rescue in most cooking situations, and I wanted to know if he thought, like I did, that this burnt sugar tasted more like blackstrap molasses. He did. He can also tell you that hot burnt sugar spilled on a bare hand and on a new T-shirt are not good combinations. He will also readily inform anyone that he'd rather watch Andrew Zimmern eat goat stomach in Namibia than watch me try to make a Martha Washington cake.

But the burn episode was not the last of his involvement in this kitchen nightmare.

My seventh mistake was in trusting a recipe that's at least 50 years old. Here I was trying my darndest to whip up a seven-minute frosting in a double boiler—a pot combination that I've only used a few times in my life, having preferred to leave that to my mother when she made the best chocolate pie in the world or the densest fudge on earth. The basic recipe was at the top of the page, while several variations were underneath. Imagine reading and re-reading the main recipe, then glancing down at the burnt-sugar version to make sure I understood the directions. When it said to place the egg whites, sugar syrup, and other ingredients in a double boiler pan but not yet on the boiling water, mix it, then place it over the water, and cook for seven minutes while beating it, that's what I did. I beat it and beat it and beat it, trying not to get the mixer cord on the burner, with one eye on the timer and another on the cookbook. About the time six minutes had passed and no firm peaks had appeared in the dang pan, I read the admonition, "Do not overcook!" Seven minutes passed and still no peaks. Eight minutes, still no peaks.

I want my mother! Where is she when I need her?! By golly, that runny seven-minute icing was going on those three layers, no matter what.

I carefully peeled the waxed paper off the three layers, plopped one on a plate, spread a little hot icing on it, plopped the second layer on, iced. Third layer on—there wasn't nearly enough icing to go on the top and sides.

Lemonade Man enters the lioness' lair and comments on what I've just noticed: the layers are totally crooked. We get a large spatula and lift the top layer off, trying to rob it of icing to cover the top of the second layer that's now had its smooth surface exposed. The result was a cake that would win the ugliest cake contest, hands down.

As I angrily scraped the top layer into the trash, tripping over a dog who loves sweets and was frantically licking up crumbs, I surveyed the results of two hours of work. In a moment of insanity, I raised my fist and threatened to smash the remains into smithereens, then broke into a tearful, "I'm never gonna cook again. We're going to eat all our meals out from now on, especially dessert!"

The eighth mistake was in trying to fix supper in between rounds of cake-baking and icing making. That pot of chili will go down in history as the absolute worst I've ever made.

With all these mistakes, there must be lessons. The primary lesson I learned is to forget about making something as good as your mom made. It ain't happenin'.

The second lesson I learned is that birthday cakes come from the store. There are many more lessons here not worth repeating, but I have learned that a bad cake tastes better with coffee and ice cream on top and that nobody said you have to eat the whole thing. *2011*

Part 6:

Laughing About Country vs. City Was John Denver Dillusional?

Backstory

I'm a country girl. Even though I spent a few years in Kansas City, from 2011 to 2018, I had to be dragged there initially against my will. Call me unsophisticated, but I come from simple people who lived close to the land and may have worked in the dirt. I enjoyed playing in the dirt and being close to nature. Sometimes that rubbed friends, husbands, and dates the wrong way.

I blame this love of country things on my mother and her rural background. She made me join 4-H, where I learned to sew, do cooking demonstrations, and enter projects in county fairs. She also made me work in our family garden, which I resented the heck out of when I was 13, but the family genes somehow found me gardening as an adult. And I was always happiest when I could look out the windows of my house at a pastoral setting.

Bullfrogs and flowers, or jazz and art . . .

Dating a man who cut his teeth on a New York apartment rooftop and later had the city of Chicago as his personal playground provides some interesting opportunities for cultural interchange.

The Mad Mother comes from a long line of people close to the land. With a name in my background like Hoffmeister (which native Germans tell me means "groundskeeper") it's no surprise that messing with flowers and lawns gives me lots of satisfaction. Thus, it follows that my idea of a fun evening is grilling burgers and serving them with new potatoes and fresh from the garden green beans, beets, and zucchini that I harvested myself. Supper out of the way, it's time to go for a drive in the country to a friend's house to pick up a bushel basket full of beets that she doesn't have time to preserve. The Kid, being a pickled beet fanatic, seems to go through a quart a month all by himself, so I scrounge for all the veggies I can find.

Even that trip in the country with a city boy showed the contrasts in attitude between them and us. He actually braked for four rabbits crossing the road in front of the car. In my calloused country disdain for the annoying creatures that eat gardens and recently caused an acquaintance a life-threatening illness, I said, "Why didn't you just run over them?" He looked at me with cool detachment and said simply, "I'm not a natural predator."

I got a chance to put him back in his place later when we were cutting off beet tops in preparation for cooking. He cut a few of the tops all the way to the beet before I shouted at him to leave an inch on them, or they'd bleed so bad we'd have anemic pickled beets.

We take our knowledge of distinct cultures for granted. I thought everybody knew that beets bled and that rabbits are nuisances. Despite these awkward moments, the city boy really likes his forays into local antique shops and the fact that everybody waves at him like they know him.

The next night, the country girl went to the city and sat in open-mouthed amazement as we drove by the gigantic sculpture of a badminton shuttlecock on the grounds of the Nelson-Atkins Museum of Art. I drooled with longing to go to the Mid-America Shakespeare Festival nearby but settled contentedly for spending three hours at the Grand Emporium listening to an awesome jazz harmonica player. The evening wound down in Johnson County, Kansas, where you can't tell a McDonald's from an apartment complex, and where flying insects are probably banned by strict zoning ordinances.

There really is a world of difference between the country and the city. Out here we place a lot of emphasis on rituals surrounding food—growing it and preserving it. Our lives revolve around friends and family, around church and community. Some of us don't spend a lot of time being entertained by anything more sophisticated than a chorus of bullfrogs and cicadas from the comfort of a lawn chair on the front porch. And if we want a feast for the eyes, all we have to do is look up at night and there are the stars and they don't compete with mercury vapor for attention.

But the city still entices. It offers a buffet for the mind. There are bookstores to spend hours in and plenty of places to buy the latest Jimmy Buffet tape. There are restaurants to sample and museums to explore. In the city you can find almost as many men wearing earrings as women. And it's not unusual to pass Nick Lowry on the freeway, identifiable by his vanity license plates.

It makes a person feel pretty fortunate to be able to have bullfrogs and flowers and fresh air to soothe your soul most of the time, but to also have noise, lights, and action just an hour away, whenever you need some extra excitement.

Didn't they make a television show about this? Maybe it's time for a re-make of Green Acres with a slight role reversal. Instead of Zsa Zsa Gabor holding a pig, I could find a city boy to hold up a dead rabbit or a bunch of beets. *July 1994*

Being selfish with ice cream

Anyone who enjoys homemade ice cream will know that you just can't help yourself when a fresh vat is made. You are required, by some unspoken rule handed down through generations, to have at least two bowls.

Lemonade Man, my new husband, so named by a friend who said he'd come into my life to rearrange the lemons I'd been handed, was so excited Sunday about the chance to use an ice cream freezer that had languished on a shelf for years. He supervised the custard preparation, and much to my dismay, insisted on three cartons of whipping cream and two quarts of half and half. That's more saturated fat than I've seen in one place in years. But a taste of the raw custard told us it would probably be worth the sins of over-indulgence.

After it was lovingly prepared with lots of attention to ratios of rock salt to crushed ice, it became the center of attention for assorted neighborhood children, dogs, and cats.

Lemonade Man became as nervous as a long-tailed cat in a room full of rocking chairs. He didn't want animal hair anywhere near his ice cream. Neither did he want kids or animals upsetting the carefully-packed bucket. And he sure as heck didn't want to give it all away. Furtively, he waited until dark and spirited the bucket indoors, where the top was pulled off and an eating orgy began.

I can see us, 25 years from now, at some Lost Arts Festival, making homemade ice cream and having a new generation ooooh and aaaah over how things used to be done in the olden days. And we still probably won't want to share. *August 1995*

How we're rationalizing a move to the country

When a woman wants something, she eventually gets it. At least that's what our husbands and significant others would say. So, I'll take full blame and responsibility for moving to the country last weekend.

For four years we've bugged area real estate agents with the same wish list many of us seem to covet—a little acreage with a pond or two, lots of beautiful trees and wildlife, and a house with a big kitchen for her and a big garage for him.

For four years the right property eluded us. When we finally found just what we wanted, it happened to be 20 minutes away from Hamilton. After agonizing, losing sleep, and backing away three times from our dream property, we took a deep breath and said, "Yes, give us debt for the rest of our earthly lives, but for Pete's sake, give this woman what she wants!"

With many regrets at leaving a place I'll always consider my hometown, we find ourselves in new, unfamiliar surroundings. As with most things in life, there are tradeoffs and sacrifices for making our dreams come true. For getting that little place in the country, I've given up a quick lunch at home and the convenience of doing a load of laundry while I'm at it. Now that we have two full floors in our house, we've learned how physically painful it is to tote loaded boxes up and down them.

For a big, dream kitchen, I've learned that meal preparation involves many more footsteps than in the past, along with such decisions as whether to move the silverware drawer closer to the stove or the dishwasher, then moving it in the middle of sautéing a minute steak.

For joining the ranks of commuters who have all that "unwind" time, I've made more trips to the gas pump.

For having the privacy of being able to go out on the deck in our underwear, we've traded waking up at midnight to unidentifiable things that go bump and squeak outside.

For having a ten-point buck and a herd of wild turkeys for new neighbors, we've said good-bye to some of the greatest people, folks who were always ready to keep an eye on our house if we had to be out of town, or who brought us a sweet potato pie fresh out of the oven.

For moving to a place that's five minutes from a taco at 9:30 p.m. if that's what we desire, I get to put up with a few jibes in Hy-Klas (where I'll continue to do my grocery shopping) from people like T. J. Adams, who insists I just want to be closer to Walmart. (NOT!)

Time will tell if we've made the mistake of our lives, but meanwhile we'll be out enjoying the woods and the creek. If you can't find us at the office, you'll know the back-to-nature freaks are out communing with wildlife. Or at least unpacking. *November 2001*

Mother Nature giveth, and she taketh, but she could do a better job on snakes

Living in the country affords us lots of opportunities to watch critters in their natural habitat. Watching the birds is more entertaining than most primetime television shows, and a lot healthier than going out to eat.

We spend many relaxing minutes each day sitting on the front porch watching the bluebirds go in and out of the wooden houses we inherited with our 15 acres.

When Lemonade Man mows pasture, he gets a closer look at some unusual critters that camp in the nearby white oaks. We may have identified a summer tanager from its attempts to keep the crows away from his mate's nest. And there are always the places you can spot from the tractor where the deer bed down under cedars. But the drawback to mowing is that you often disturb the habitat a little too much. During the last mowing, Lemonade Man didn't see a rabbit's home until he saw blood and fur on his tires. He nearly threw up, especially when he saw a hawk swoop down minutes later to consume the pasture kill.

Now he's become used to all sorts of birds following his brush cutter, waiting for what the blades might destroy. Still, he tries to be careful, leaving clumps of tall grass around a quail's nest, which Mama Quail later abandons anyway.

The cycle of life and death that we get closer to in the country usually carries a kind of harsh poetic justice and balance. But we decided last week that we'd intervene a little more than usual in the natural pattern.

It was all because of our favorite finch. She had kept us company every time we stepped out our back door, scolding us imperiously from the ceramic birdhouse that she'd built a nest in for the second year in a row. For a day or so we'd missed her chirping. We were eyeing the poison oak climbing the tree her house hung from when I looked in the entrance.

"That's no bird," I told Lemonade Man. I insisted the matter be investigated, and it was—with a stick. The pattern-not-like-a-bird moved, sliding sideways. That's when I went berserk, realizing that Mother Nature had just inflicted a terrible and ugly cruelty.

I got sent to the house for the pellet gun by a man more afraid of snakes than I ever thought about being. He stuck the barrel into the opening to the house and blasted away, sending shards of pottery flying in the air. After the third shot, a juvenile snake dropped out of the bird house, dripping blood and striking. It was a copperhead.

A hoe dispatched the still-striking reptile, whose carcass was banished to the woods from whence it came. Now we know why the dogs refused to step one foot off the patio.

The snake had managed to kill the mother finch and her babies. Maybe this is why none of the other birdhouses on the place had been built in this year. Could be they were inhabited with the ghosts of departed bird souls killed by snakes.

The incident wouldn't have been so traumatic if it hadn't been followed by just a few days by another encounter with a reptile, a six-foot rattlesnake that lost its tail in the mower. Big Guy got charged with disposing of the still-living creature by throwing it over the fence with a hoe. Only trouble was, it boomeranged back at his feet, hissing as it landed. Never saw that kid move so fast. The crows finally finished the job, pecking, then quickly hopping out of striking range.

Friends who have heard the snake stories only make matters worse with their comments like, "Where there are two snakes there are others," and, "Do you have any idea how many snakes there are per acre?" A neighbor added his two cents worth, noting, "Didn't you know your place is called Rattlesnake Bluff?"

We can only hope that there's no such thing as poisonous snake revenge, or we'll be putting up a for-sale sign soon. *June 2003*

Mailbox bashing—rites of country initiation

Just because we live in the country, we would never presume to be called farm folks. You can't row crop 15 acres of hills and timber and snakes. Sure, we could have horses or cows grazing on that nice fescue and red clover, but then we'd have to contend with manure on our car tires, and eventually in the basement garage.

So, we're just used-to-be-town dwellers squatting on a parcel of land that would probably be better used by someone with real farm dirt in their veins. Still, we joined the fraternity of real rural dwellers last weekend when we had our mailbox vandalized.

It was such a pretty thing, too—white with two deer on the side and the number of our 911 address perched proudly on top. Yes, mailbox vanity is something we succumbed to. It sort of makes a statement about who you are and what you value. We like watching the deer on our "farm." And I had just bought a snazzy new magnetic cover with a colorful tribute to bluebirds on it before a baseball bat-wielding young person had his jollies in a Saturday night free-for-all.

Our neighbor is a John Deere fanatic, and his mailbox is a green tractor. His personal identity statement didn't get smashed. We know, since we took the long way to town Saturday morning, doing an inventory, because the sheriff's dispatcher had asked if anyone else had damage on our road. Our inventory showed several boxes knocked askew, one knocked off its block and others dinged and pitted.

When we moved in, the previous owners had said their mailbox got knocked down twice by the snowplow, so they gave up and got a post office box. Now we wonder.

Other rural dwellers, knowing that the mailbox bashers will never be caught, have developed some ingenious coping strategies. One of our neighbors has an elaborate shield of hog wire surrounding his mailbox. Another had his in a CCA frame that a baseball bat would ricochet off of before it ever reached the metal box.

We're thinking of electrifying ours. Now, all we need to come up with is a way to not electrocute the mail carrier, while hoping that the baseball bat being used for bashing is one of those heavy metal ones.

So, let's see—snakes, weeds, mailbox bashing. Did I mention the distinctive odor of ether when the wind's just right that could presage a meth lab? Thank God I'm a country girl. I think. *June 2003*

Plagues of plenty in the heartland: John Denver had it all wrong

Every time we go to the garden in 95-degree heat, Lemonade Man says, "We're not gonna do this next year."

I'm willing to make concessions in my love of fresh veggies. For example, it might be okay next year to only plant three rows of corn instead of eight, two zucchini plants instead of four, four tomatoes instead of eight. We've already downsized from 18 tomato plants and eight zucchini last year, so we're making progress.

We're also streamlining our garden operations, thanks to some new technology. Planting this year didn't involve bending over and dropping each seed in the ground. We just went to Orscheln's and bought a handy-dandy planter that makes the furrow, drops the seed in the ground, covers it up with a chain and even marks the next row—all in one pass over the field.

The latest gardening innovation was the purchase of a $26 plastic cart from Walmart. I sit on the thing and push myself down the green bean row, stashing the harvest in the hole and never bending over. The same cart is a lot easier to get to the house for canning the produce instead of carrying five-gallon buckets.

Despite such improvements, there's no getting around having to stay up until midnight watching a canner do its job. Or trying to figure out what to do with all this zucchini.

When my brothers came here from Texas two weeks ago, they drove past our driveway and ended up on a gravel road a few miles away. The couple they asked directions of obliged, but the price of getting un-lost was to relieve the two of their excess cucumbers and zucchini.

Why do we burden ourselves with gardens? What errant gene makes us feel guilty unless we're toiling in the hot sun trying to coax vegetable fiber out of the ground? We always excuse it with the reminder that sweet corn frozen in July will taste mighty good in January. But is a permanent crick in the back worth it?

In rural America, we're plagued with plenty. Amend that. In America in general, most of us have more than our fair share of everything we need. Yeah, yeah, we know. It's a distribution problem, getting the food to the people who need it the most.

That philosophical problem aside, we're thinking of having a Children of the Corn party this weekend. We hope to sucker some of our city friends into coming out and helping us harvest and freeze our sweet corn in exchange for a barbecue. Of course, we'll neglect to tell them that they'll have to squeeze between rows that are only 18" apart and full of weeds and ticks.

I'm just glad this isn't World War II when the war office set a quota of 120 cans of fruit, vegetables, or meat for each person. You were doomed if you had a big family and had to can 120 times each member.

Ahhh! Life in the country! John Denver was nuts. *July 2003*

Now, about this hunting stuff . . .

There are good things and there are bad things about the swarm of gun-toting folks dressed in camo that will be descending on gas stations, liquor stores, and restaurants this weekend to see if they can bring home a Bambi trophy.

The good things are the previously-mentioned hunting dollars that will be spent locally. The bad things might include a few rotten eggs that spoil the reputation of the sport—things like trigger-happy novices, possibly fueled with a little extra octane, opening up on anything that moves in a field, like a farmer's hogs or cows.

On our 15 wooded acres, we've enjoyed watching deer and turkey roam around and chew on our white oak acorns. We've witnessed seven young turkeys grow from little butterballs waddling behind their mother, with the dad keeping a watchful eye from the rear, to full size birds with beards. We considered them our wild pets.

So, it was with a lot of chagrin that we caught some young boys on our driveway a few weeks ago, trying to flush out the two birds that remained after some other uninvited guests bagged them on our property and bragged about it at the check station.

After Lemonade Man put the fear of God and landowners into the youngsters, uninviting them from our driveway, we hurriedly did what we should have done when we moved in—posted a no hunting sign.

Not that it will do any good. We've heard some hunters take special delight in tearing up the signs. Still, I'm sure the majority of hunters are law-abiding and respectful of property rights.

Yes, we know that deer are overpopulating this area. We live in dread of running into one with our front bumper on the way home from work this time of year. Still, we admire the magnificence of some of God's most beautiful creatures.

Last Saturday I heard the sound of heavy leaf and branch rustling from the woods behind our house and went to the door to see what was causing the commotion. A doe came running into the yard, followed several yards behind by a proud ten-point buck. As he followed her into another part of the woods, he pranced like a Tennessee walking horse in the show ring, hooves held high and head even higher. Soon I saw the cause of their running. Two Australian shepherd dogs came out of the woods, close on their heels, until I hollered at them to go home. They did and we all lived happily ever after, until bullets started whizzing by and we had to holler down the hill "There's a house up here, you idiots!"

Selfishly, and in a city kind of way, we want these animals for our own pleasure. We want to name them and talk to them and have them feed out of our hands. But we know that's not nature's way. I know of many people who depend on venison to feed their families. Indeed, when I was growing up, it was nothing for my own single mother to head out the door with her gun in search of a squirrel or a rabbit. I learned to pick shot out of my meat and not complain, because we were lucky to have meat on the table, even if it was a tough old thing, simmered in Madeira wine to make it palatable. That was, and is, the country way. *November 2003*

Of mice and men and their pickup trucks

Well, we've been officially initiated into the good ole boys club. The mouse club, that is.

This passage into being dubbed a By-Gosh Country Couple had its genesis in finding the plug to the firewall of the pickup lying on the floorboard. That led to Lemonade Man wondering when he'd last eaten licorice in the truck. There were little black sprinkles in the stitching of the truck seat. We scratched our heads in puzzlement over the two incidents, never imagining their underlying cause.

The morning after those discoveries, the mystery unraveled with the appearance of two dazed and ugly baby mice on the floorboard of the truck. Further investigation revealed they had been brought into this world with the help of shavings from the blanket we keep under the back fold-down seat. Nice little nest!

If I had been the one to make the discovery, you would have heard a scream all the way to the interstate. As it was, the man who can't bear to harm any creature (unless it's a snake) tenderly scooped the baby mice into a dustpan and tossed them into the yard. On second thought, he covered them with a cluster of leaves in hopes their mother would discover them and rescue them to breed more of their kind somewhere normal and countryfied, like the barn or woodpile.

He then watched their slow and agonizing death over the next two days, uncovering them to check their progress and finally pronouncing them gone with guilty acknowledgement that at least they died in each other's arms. Meanwhile, it was time to buy a trap to set in the truck to see if any siblings survived. That might have worked if I hadn't set it off with a bag of groceries that landed on top of it.

Now we're after the D-con® and hoping that any leftover critters don't die in some inaccessible place, only to be found during an oil change.

In one of his forays into the usual realms of farmer types, Lemonade Man learned that mice building nests in a pickup is more the rule than the exception. He was told that he didn't want to leave his door open if he had occasion to take the truck to the pasture. That's when the ingenious mouse will climb up into the cab and set up housekeeping. He was told he was lucky. It could have been a squirrel that decided to adopt a new house on wheels.

And so, we move more into veteran status as country dwellers, past mailbox bashings, snake killings, and fighting a never-ending battle against moles who eat our sweet potatoes. We've graduated from mud daubers building nests in the brake shoes of our sports car to mice in our pickup. We have earned our country scout badges.

Unfortunately, it didn't stop with the mouse. We got home on Sunday from a long-anticipated weekend in the city to discover a power outage that began probably the minute we drove out of the driveway. After noting the dripping water under the freezer, we called the power company. The lineman tore himself away from the Chiefs game and had the power back on in a few minutes. The cause? A squirrel had gotten into a fuse on the main power pole.

Was it just a little twist of irony that we had gone to Kansas City to see our first-ever opera, *Of Mice and Men? November 18, 2004*

We lost the Great Gopher War of 2006

With Groundhog Day quickly nipping at our heels, we can't even think about the potential predictor of spring. The furry beast that occupies our psyche is a relative of Puxatawnie Phil. We call him Gomer the Gopher and his Whole Goldern Family. They're living in the white oak tree in our front yard and won't vacate, despite the many eviction notices we've given them.

Now, some conservation-minded folks would say they've paid their rent by aerating the soil for us. That would be fine and dandy if, in the process of aerating, they didn't leave five mounds a day on the surface of our pampered, fertilized, grub-free lawn.

As usual, when we face what for us is a certifiable farm crisis, we head to the local co-op store, where old timers seem to lie in wait for a gullible former city dweller.

When Lemonade Man arrived in said store the other day, as he was paying for another round of poison peanuts, he was accosted by an overalled gentleman with a knowing twinkle in his eye, who commented slyly, "You're a city boy, aren't you?"

Upon getting an affirmative, embarrassed nod, the old timer said, "You know, you're just feeding those critters. Now, the thing you need to do is level off those gopher hills, then find the main tunnel. Have you got a garden hose close by?"

"Yes."

"Well, what you do is, you stick that hose down the main tunnel and turn the water on. Let it flow gently for at least an hour. You may have to do it a few days in a row, but you should get them to move on by drowning their children and making it too muddy for them to tunnel."

Don't tell PETA, but the old timer's instructions were followed to the letter. We're now on our fifth try of flooding gopher tunnels. Persistent little critters, they are! There are still new pop-ups every morning around the old oak tree. We're now beginning to wonder if that old-timer is on the rural water board and they're just needing to increase their revenues.

Lemonade Man is now becoming leery of seeking any more advice at the co-op store. We may get desperate enough in the gopher wars to follow Kenneth Simpson's method. He poured gasoline in his mole runs then set them on fire. *January 2006*

Getting in a rhubarb about shrews and trapped squirrels

Frank and Margie Kromeich brought us some rhubarb from their garden this week. I was delighted and immediately began washing and slicing it up to freeze. Lemonade Man was less than enthusiastic.

City boy doesn't like the looks of this plant. He's never tried it solo but always with strawberries. Last night, I made him try some rhubarb sauce over cottage cheese. I've found that most diabetics like anything sugary, so he tried it and liked it. Half an hour later he wanted to know why his mouth was so puckery and dry.

On a website devoted to all kinds of trivia about rhubarb, you can learn that this plant is high in fiber and a good source of vitamin C. Its strange character is probably the reason that the third definition of rhubarb is that of a heated discussion or argument.

It was almost a rhubarb we had at our house Saturday night.

In replacing a tree that had died last year, a landscape man took a look at our dying creeping juniper and immediately announced the presence of shrews, or at least some very hungry mice. He suggested setting some mouse traps and baiting them with peanut butter. We obeyed. Then we got ready to take away their food source.

The minute it stopped raining Sunday, we spent three hours tugging, cutting, and hauling off sticky evergreens. In the process, we uncovered the shrew or mouse burrow and situated the traps close by. Our efforts were rewarded with one critter caught in the wooden mouse trap.

But we caught another critter entirely in the live trap we also baited with peanut butter. And that's where the rhubarb almost developed. After returning from Kansas City, where we spent the day visiting relatives, we noticed some unusual activity and noise from the patio. Something was in the live trap.

There was Pool Boy, captured by his newly-discovered love for peanut butter.

This critter we've learned to cuss, this animal that has cost us scraped arms and hands from installing hardware cloth and chicken wire around all our garden containers—finally snared! We were elated.

That is, until we saw how scared the poor critter was. Instead of peppering him through the cage with the pellet gun Lemonade Man had bought especially with his name on it, we decided to take him to a new, faraway spot, considering for a moment inside the city limits, to pay back all those city folks who dump dogs at our driveway. But no, that wouldn't do.

Matter of fact, I got to feeling sorry for the panicky little creature, caught by his own weakness for goodies. I told Lemonade Man that if we took him very far off, he would be totally despondent and suffer severe psychological effects.

Being tender-hearted where animals are concerned, Lemonade Man complied. We released him and watched him run sideways to the woods in his hasty retreat. We figured that, just maybe, the scare of being in a metal cage for a few hours would make him associate the patio with danger and he'd avoid us like the plague.

Monday night, there was Pool Boy, sitting contentedly on the steps to the deck, calmly eating an acorn.

Well, at least it wasn't an onion or a strawberry plant.

I wonder if squirrels like frozen rhubarb. *2007*

The invasion of spring and the Angus steers

We're getting our annual dose of the winter tease, that time when we're allowed to get a brief reminder of what we anxiously await every January and February. We're talking shirtsleeves weather that makes you crazy to get out and dig in the dirt, wash windows, and rake up the rest of the fall leaves, go fishing and take a drive with the car windows down and your head stuck out.

That February, spring fever must have struck the 200 head of Black Angus steers our neighbor runs across the fence from our place.

Way down in the brush, next to a deep ravine, a tree fell on the fence that separates us from our rancher neighbor. His livestock played Follow-the-Leader down by our frog pond, up the hill to our corral, and right into our front yard.

We had been to Kansas City, and I dropped Lemonade Man off at the top of the driveway to get some exercise walking to the house while I ran to the store for eggs and milk. He called on his cell phone a few minutes later and said excitedly, "Houston, we have a situation here!" He was in the process of counting black blobs of livestock flesh and lost track at 35. He began practicing his farmer voice, yelling "Hyerre cow, hyerre cow!" Not sure where he got that particular call, but the steers were not buying it. They ran.

By the time he got to the house, he began counting cow piles, then noticed large hoof prints all over the yard, then saw the nozzle on the gas tank had been knocked off. From the river rock scattered out of the landscaping at the front of the house and onto the front patio, and the four solar lights that been mowed down, it looked like the spring steers had walked up and rung the front doorbell.

We thought the mailbox bashing and mailbox explosion last year had been our baptism by fire as rural residents. Now we know that you have not truly experienced life in the rural lane until the cows come to your front door. *March 2009*

Part 7:

Laughing About Growing Older and Adapting to New Technology

Backstory

As most of us hit our golden years, we do so with lots of resistance. Our brains lie to us and lead us to believe we can do at age 50 what we once did at 30. The theme of aging brain cells and worn-out bodies carried me through many humor columns; from adapting to a CPAP machine to getting my first colonoscopy to starting another new diet to searching for the ultimate wrinkle cream.

Besides adapting to the challenges of aging, one of our biggest issues in the newspaper business and life at large was (and still is) adapting to new technology. While publishing a newspaper, we learned to surf the internet, get our computer terminals to talk to each other, and even how to enter an online classroom as I began working on a master's degree in communications, the first of its kind in the country.

My Motorcycle Mama

It had been a few months since I'd been to visit my mother. Nothing prepared me for what I was about to see.

The same woman who is tense with worry every time she rides in a car with another driver besides herself, the same person who had to down three beers before she tried to water ski, that very same person is now driving a motorcycle to work every day.

I watched open-mouthed as she donned her shiny helmet, hitched up her Lee Riders, and straddled a shiny new Honda 250. The actions of his 56-year-old grandmother had my son muttering, "Mom, Grandma's silly!"

She is pretty silly over her new toy. She bought it because it has pretty designs on the gas tank and because the shocks look like they're made of gold.

I'd have loved being around when she taught herself how to maneuver the thing. She learned by reading the instruction manual and practicing in the gravelly, bumpy yard of their south Missouri home. My stepfather laughed so hard in describing her motorcycle education that he can barely recount the tale. It seems that she didn't want to take her feet off the ground. The faster she went, the longer her steps got. I guess you had to be there.

I was all prepared to worry about her safety, but then I followed her in the car and learned that this Motorcycle Granny takes no chances.

I can't even berate her for going through her second childhood. She and my stepdad will be hitting the road with their fifth-wheel trailer one of these days (if she can be talked into retiring from her job) and they've already had a motorcycle mount put on it. When their wanderings take them to a campsite, they'll unload the toys and go buy groceries and do some sightseeing.

Suddenly, senior citizenhood doesn't look half bad. Maybe by the time I reach it, I'll be brave enough to learn to jump horses and go hang gliding. That's my version of motorcycling. *September 1987*

Just how dumb is a box of rocks?

I didn't realize how much I'd soaked up some quaint little sayings from the extended family I married into until I wrote an advertising headline for the paper this week that no one in the office understood.

So, with apologies to Alden Hardware, as the headline was written for them, here is the questionable gem: Get a lantern charge on spring!

None of my young staffers had ever heard of a lantern charge. Probably because they never had to get up before dawn and go milk a cow with the aid of a lantern.

Neither did I, but I've heard it so often over the past 20 years, it's now a part of my routine dialogue.

We're starting to call them "Grandma-isms." It was the late matriarch of the family who was fond of quoting such witticisms as, "she's dumber than a bucket of hair," or, "poor as Job's turkey with one feather in his tail." But she didn't have a monopoly on quaint expressions.

The Old Indian tries to calm a hurt grandchild with the admonition, "I've had worse places on my lip and never quit whistling." He also compares eating angel food cake or whipped Jell-0 to, "sitting on a fence eating fog."

And who can remember a time it's been so cold it would freeze the horns off a brass monkey? There's another cruder version of that expression not fit for publication.

And who knows what a "trade last" is? Somebody gave me one a few years ago. Took me a few more years to figure out it was a compliment. It supposedly originated with trading compliments and who gave whom a compliment last. Does that make sense?

I doubt that modern American language will ever approach the early 20th century for colorful expressions. Kids these days probably won't be able to work those old things into their slang. But long after the words "awesome" and "radical" fade from use as quickly as the television mutant creatures that use them today, we'll still be able to get a chuckle out of someone making a lantern charge. That is, if we continue to respect and appreciate our language and its history.
March 1990

From cabin fever to spring fever to car sick

The Mad Mother comes from a long line of carsick people. Research surely would indicate the sickness is a trait carried in some recessive gene. I can just imagine my German and Welsh ancestors urping over the sides of wagon wheels.

My mother is still prone to the malady, so much so that when she goes anywhere, she has to either drive or ride in the front seat.

My first memory of motion sickness is a vivid one. We had just come from my aunt's wedding. I think I was the flower girl, and I had leaned over in the car to tell my mom I wasn't feeling too good and lost my wedding cake and punch all over the front seat.

That incident was followed by years of having to roll down the windows for fresh air and trying other tricks, like ingesting salty foods to stem to tide of stomach eruptions in moving vehicles.

I think Brazil cured me of carsickness. After riding in South American buses and taxis, over mountainous roads, and on one particularly harrowing ride while standing in a crowded bus filled with chickens and unwashed bodies and fighting a bad case of dysentery, I can still see myself running on a dirt road through a sugar cane field to get to my own outdoor privy, barely in time.

After that, the ole stomach must have decided it didn't have it so bad riding in American vehicles on Midwestern roads. Now, I can even read a novel and crochet in the car without getting queasy.

Not so The Kid. He's inherited the family curse, and we go nowhere further than 50 miles without our supply of Dramamine. Like a dog marking his territory, this offspring has marked several roadside spots with his breakfast or lunch. When he's suffering, my empathy gland really kicks in and I cast sidelong dirty looks at the driver for taking a curve too sharply or applying the brakes too hard when the back seat passenger is beginning to turn green.

During last year's summer vacation trip to Eureka Springs, we had the privilege of having two 11-year-olds prone to car sickness. Boy, was that fun!

Well, the fun just got funner. Last weekend we took the pups to see Grandma in Kansas City. Lemonade Man always likes to drive through Swope Park because it's scenic. It's also got some dandy curves. Years ago, when he was driving a Porsche, sans kid or Lhasa Apsos, he took them plenty fast. He couldn't feel my glare boring a hole in the side of his head this weekend. Otherwise, he would have looked down in time to see one of our critters turning green under her white fur. She lost her breakfast pancake near the entrance to Starlight Theater. She repeated her performance on the way home. Lemonade Man has promised not to go to Grandma's house through Swope Park ever again.

And now that you've reached the end of this sickening saga, I hope you're not eating breakfast or lunch. Maybe you'll excuse the grossness of the subject and make allowances for people prone to

motion sickness, who also obviously suffer from a lack of couth.
February 1996

How to melt fat naturally . . . from your fingers

Someday I'll be able to write a book about weight loss and exercise. Why? Because I've bought every book ever published on the subject.

Lemonade Man says I'm obsessed. "Why don't you just shut your mouth and push away from the table instead of buying all these books?" he wonders.

Like others of my ilk, I keep believing book jacket hype about this being the last diet I'll ever go on because it is the antidote to all the fad diets that have come before it.

Remember the thigh cruncher? That As-Seen-on-TV gadget was a device of improbable plastic and foam that you supposedly wedged between your knees. While working the spring-loaded thingamabob and watching television at the same time, you were supposed to watch the inches melt away. The only thing I ever managed to do with it was make it fly up in my face.

The thigh cruncher had the same garage sale fate as its predecessor, whose name I can't recall. It was a series of two plastic ropes on pulleys. You hooked it to your doorknob and when you pulled on the rope with your arm, your corresponding leg came up. Amazing! But it didn't show much in the way of results either.

Then we had something called the Ab Roller. It involved two of the cutest little plastic platforms designed to be used for crunches and tightening the buttocks. You just had to figure out how to make your hands follow the rolling platforms far enough to do some good but not so far that you collapsed on your face with the wheels running away from you entirely. We found the best use of the Ab Roller was in moving heavy furniture.

Now, I am not the only person in this house to succumb to purchases aimed at magically melting away inches and pounds. Lemonade Man thought that maybe two miserable, overweight souls could benefit from a Nordic Track WalkFit, that non-motorized version of the treadmill that costs more than its electric cousin just because of its trademark. It made me feel like I was actually learning to cross-country ski, but when you don't use a machine for anything but a coat rack, it doesn't do much for you.

The only things that have ever worked for the Mad Mother have been a daily trek up a steep hill, twice a day, back in the day when I was teaching in Brazil. Oh, and the roller blades I used with a portable tape player and some Michael Bolton music to spur me on.

There are no steep hills in my life now except for our three weekly deadlines. And the tennis courts where the roller blades were used is full of treacherous cracks. Excuses, excuses.

These days, our weight loss is still confined to the latest fads. We've been the Matabolife route (it gave me diarrhea), and not long ago we ordered a New Age regimen of amaranth seeds, rice milk, and colon purging teas. Not exactly palate-pleasing to someone raised on meat, potatoes, bread, and one vegetable every meal, preferably fried.

The last thing I bit on was a video by a 53-year-old bombshell. This bearer of three ten-pound offspring, who once weighed 250 (or so she claims), asserts that simply by breathing deeply while doing isometric and isotonic floor exercises, you can watch the fat literally melt away. Imagine a Farrah Fawcett look-alike in a skimpy leotard, breathing like a truck driver playing basketball, and making a grimace like a lion as she demonstrates how to give yourself a natural facelift. The really crazy thing is, she got me to do it too. Every morning.

So far, the main result of this new regimen has been to bring the dogs and cat running to see if I'm sick because of all the heavy wheezing. Once they determine I'm okay, they coil themselves around my arms and legs, ready to play, licking my face while I have my leg in the air and my arms disabled.

The only other thing I've noticed about deep wheezing is that I'm losing weight in my fingers. *October 21, 1998*

How to take advantage of modern bra technology

Buying a bra in the new millennium is not as simple as it used to be. Technology has complicated the process.

On a dreary Sunday afternoon, Mad Mother and Lemonade Man headed to the mall with only two purchases in mind—a few bras for me and one or two pair of shoes, also for me (nothing for him, as he uses catalogs and the bargain bins at Orscheln's for his shopping).

While I headed to the Big Mama section of a well-known department store, in search of something ugly without underwires and little or no padding, my better half stayed around the checkout counter trying to look inconspicuous, as he was the only male within a 40-mile radius. As is his usual pattern of seeking entertainment, he struck up a conversation with a salesclerk. Then it must have hit him that he needed to go on a mission of mercy for a relative who is not exactly generously endowed.

Someone should have filmed the conversation, or at least the hand gestures, as he tried to solicit information that would help this relative buy a bra to make her look a little more alluring. It was his lucky day. The salesclerk was neither offended, nor was she at a loss for words. Matter of fact, she was quite frank in referring to her own physique with the terms "balloons that have lost their air" after nursing seven children.

But she sympathized with my husband's dilemma in trying to assist his under-endowed relative. She showed him a product that looked like something I wore in high school as the top of a two-piece bathing suit. Of course it had those tortuous underwires that can cut a woman in two by 3:30 p.m. But in addition to that uplifting aid, it had a little secret pocket inside. In that pocket, you could stuff an entire shoulder pad, with the idea being that what couldn't sink down would have to ooze out on top. Problem solved.

She did, however, have another alternative. She called it the water bra and said a person could buy one at Walmart for $15 or less. It works on the same principle as the first product, except that in place of material and cotton, you use water. And you can use as much water as you want. The advantage here is that the water doesn't slosh or anything and doesn't feel artificial in case someone should accidentally grab you. That's good to know.

So, we got an education in bra buying. And I thought I'd learned all there was to learn until Lemonade Man noted later that night, "Did you know you can get a bra extender, so that if you're really a size 40, you can buy a 38 and it will still fasten around you?" Wish that worked with slacks too. Then I'd start buying size twelves again and brag about it. *November 2002*

Pass the fat-free cereal, please

Modern man and woman is doomed.

If the stress generated by fighting with computers all day doesn't kill us, lipstick will.

Today's daily headline screamed that there are carcinogens in lipstick, shaving cream, fingernail polish, and shampoo. And nobody's protecting us against them.

My big fear is guar gum. Xantham gum is my second leading cause of nightmares. About 20 years ago, while enjoying some fattening confection with Cool Whip, I happened to read the ingredients. "What the heck is guar gum?" I wondered aloud. It sounded inedible and undigestible and ever since that day, I swear I belch and have heartburn every time I eat a Jell-O salad topped with the stuff. You'd think the aversion would lead to abstinence, but no church or family dinner is complete without some generous dollops of Cool-Whip.

Seriously, what are they putting in our food, let alone our cosmetics? We are such a faddish culture that whatever health study catches the headlines, we tailor our buying habits to counteract the trouble.

Years ago, we rushed out to buy the "lite" versions of our favorite foods. That gave way to low-fat or no-fat and the trend to be an educated American and read nutrition labels. But food companies undoubtedly have hired accountants turned labelers, because they hide the truth on those labels by playing tricks on our non-mathematical minds. They tell us there are so many grams of cholesterol and fat in a serving and then in tiny print tell us that there are four servings in a package. Or worse, they print the ingredients in four-point type so you have to go get the magnifying glass to read it.

Have you ever read a list of ingredients out loud? You'd have to have an advanced degree in nutrition science or in lexicology to even be able to pronounce the words. That could be the next board game to sweep the nation. Instead of *Trivial Pursuit* or *How to Become a Millionaire* it will be *How to Read Nutrition Labels*. This game would give you points for correct pronunciation of ingredients, allow you to advance through the stomach and intestines on the game board with little side visits to the capillaries and liver to see what damage those ingredients could do to each part of your body.

When I get done deciphering the labels on the high fiber bread we just bought and wondering why in the world it never molds, I might get around to inventing this board game. But right now, I'm writing a scathing letter to my favorite cereal company complaining about the insult they give to me every time they label a box of cereal "no-fat." How dumb does the cereal industry think we are? (Don't answer that if you've ever given in to a request by your child to buy a cereal based on its television advertisement.) *March 2005*

Advice for the technologically challenged: Polish your shoes

Lemonade Man has been finding great satisfaction on recent dark fall evenings by dragging out his leather shoes and boots and polishing them. He applies the polish, rubs it in, lets it sit a few minutes, and brings out the shine with a soft shoe brush.

I get the same satisfaction in cleaning and rearranging the cans in the kitchen pantry. It doesn't take a lot of smarts to put the vegetables on one side of the shelf and the fruits on the other, and stack them all a little more neatly than when I was tired from grocery shopping and just threw them in any old way. You'd think I'd learn to put them away correctly to begin with, but then, where would my satisfaction at doing a simple task come from?

The more our lives become ruled and overwhelmed by technology, the more we will yearn for simpler tasks that don't frustrate and challenge us.

Big Guy came home from college one recent weekend and did us the favor of taking out all the connections to our electronic devices and reinstalling them in a supposedly more logical and easier-to-use pattern. Now, instead of the satellite TV, the DVD, and VCR going through the VCR, they all go through the surround sound system. To a young mind, that made more sense. We accepted his word as gospel, knowing that 20-somethings are more adept at this sort of thing. But we failed to get written, explicit, step-by-step instructions. We still can't get the system to play a VCR tape or a DVD movie unless we accidentally push the right combination of buttons. Big Guy assures us that our problems will be solved by the installation of a signal box that all these devices can talk to. We're hoping said device will appear under our Christmas tree.

Every workday we fight computers and realize that the little we know about software and hardware is just enough to make us dangerous. We skirt the edge of disaster with equipment that's obsolete the moment it comes out. We marvel at our colleagues who seem to know all the ins and outs of various programs and the bells and whistles they produce. And we understand why some of our older acquaintances refuse to even touch a computer, let alone try to program a satellite receiver or a police scanner.

I overheard Lemonade Man talking today with a cell phone representative. They were discussing something called "bluetooth" that we are really going to need in the future to stay on top of our lives.

"What was all that about?" I asked when he got off the phone. "I don't have a clue," he responded.

We're going to have to find more comforting routines that will allow us to unwind from our confrontations with a world that is quickly superseding and surpassing us. We can only hope that everyone who is electronically challenged has their own version of shoe polishing and pantry cleaning and access to younger minds that can plug the gaps. *November 2005*

Feeling like a one-legged woman in a rear-kicking contest

Is there any more electronic technology a person could crowd into a busy day? I'm beginning to feel like the proverbial one-legged woman in a rear-kicking contest.

I just realized that after inserting two new cartridges in an ink jet printer while waiting for a photo to finish going through cyberspace to its intended recipient, I used the time efficiently to text message Big Guy, after which I inserted a flash drive into the PC on my desk to transfer files from it to the Macintosh computer on my sidebar. Heaven forbid that the phone ring in the middle of any of this or the left hand will forget what the right hand was assigned.

I had it coming, since I skipped out entirely on a full day of rewiring the four television sets at home. While Lemonade Man and Big Guy traced wires and clipped and snipped, talking about splitters, coaxial, and quick-connects, I indulged in some old-fashioned technology by reading a book. For that, I earned peace of mind and expanded horizons, while the boys got frazzled. And their work continued long after Big Guy returned to his city apartment with a frantic call from Lemonade Man that the LCD TV no longer has audio. Our electronic guru walked through installing a different connection over the phone so we could have sound to go along with our Hallmark TV special.

I'm thinking of advocating a day when we all opt out of electronic tasking. Do you suppose it would be possible not to turn on the computer, the television, the microwave, or use a cell phone for one day? I wonder how much our moods would lift? Would we find a huge void in our routine that could only be filled by a renewed bout of googling and checking emails? Would we have to revert to (heaven forbid) face-to-face human contact?

How many times have you asked yourself, after playing email tag with a friend or associate, "Why in the world don't I just pick up the phone and set a date for a meeting?"

About the fourth time I sent a text message to Big Guy, I forwarded one last missive, "Wouldn't it just be easier to have voice contact?" The reply I got back was, "Gee mom, you really make me laugh."

If terrorists want to bring us to our knees as a nation, all they'll have to do is shut down cyberspace and knock out our cell towers. I'm sure they're working on that right now. We can only hope there are some old-timers who know how to do business on typewriters. Now, how funny is that?! *2009*

Feet don't fail me now!

Lemonade Man has been entertaining the extended family for decades with his storytelling abilities. When things get a little dull, or when winter threatens to hang on way too long, he pulls things out of his mental file cabinet and begins to practice his art.

This must be an inherited trait, undoubtedly from the Native American side of the family. His sister has the gift too. Both of them add dramatic embellishments and elaborate hand gestures to their tales. Lemonade Man always throws in sound effects for good measure and changes his voice to fit the character he's portraying.

His file of stories contains one called "Escaping from Women" that details how he extricated himself from scary entanglements. One of the tamer ones features a woman he thought was a good fishing buddy pleading with him to stay at her house. As he was pulling out of her driveway, she was hanging onto the door of the truck, begging him to reconsider. His pat quotation in such predicaments is, "I've got to go now," with a whispered, "feet don't fail me now!"

Even today, just to make me a little jealous, this storyteller will regale me with tales of all the women at cosmetic counters who flirt with him while he's buying me a gift. Yesterday, he had a 72-year-old widow from Florida proposition him while he was trying to buy some Tupelo honey from her over the phone. She wanted to know if he had a full head of hair, then if he was single. Her daughter was in the background yelling at her to, "stop that!"

Through the years I feel like I've personally met all the characters he used to work with or the neighbors he used to visit—from the woman who used to sit on her front porch in her bra because the younger girls walked the neighborhood in their two-piece swimsuits, to the hard-drinking couple that fought over the last beer until the man ended up without the beer but with a new black eye.

His humorous escapades, that I often steal and put in this space, have become legendary to our readers. So much so, that when the girls in the mailing room at the printer's recently discovered he was the real Lemonade Man, they gave him a standing ovation. They told him their favorite story was the time he was washing the car and lost control of the washing wand and his pants fell to the ground.

The last time I spoke to Ben Harper, a few years before his death, he told me flat out, "If I was your husband, I'd have divorced you by now for telling all those stories." But Ben was a veteran storyteller himself, so he might have just been jealous of somebody having such a public forum for tales. *2009*

When I am old, I shall wear triple hydrating essential oil of curdled milk

You know you're getting old when you spend a whole day with a girlfriend visiting cosmetic counters at the mall to find just the right wrinkle cream.

Chris and I went to high school together, rode the same bus, cut each other's hair, and tee-peed a teacher's house on Halloween. She stood up with me at my wedding and I stood up with her at two out of three of hers. She's one of those people you could love to hate because they stay petite, cute, and slim and are still teaching aerobics at age 43.

But we said to heck with petite and slim on Saturday as we pigged out on Mexican cuisine, then attacked the mall for some serious spring shopping. Or, rather, it attacked us.

Every single cosmetic counter in that place had hordes of commission-hungry saleswomen giving away free samples. Their sales pitches came fast and furious, if you even looked halfway interested. Being a saleswoman of sorts myself, I threw them off balance by complimenting their technique before breezing away and not buying a $50 pot of the lightest, most hydrating cream in the world.

By the end of the day, we had not a spot on our persons free of some fragrance or lotion. I got suckered into buying a $32 bottle of perfume (but only because it came with a "free" gift valued at $105) and a tube of lipstick that was essential for my winter "Color Me Beautiful" coloring.

Chris bought the latest beauty item—something about essential fruits and acids—made with curdled milk and orange peels and guaranteed to make your skin softer and smoother.

The cosmetic industry and the consumers of their products are something a sociologist really ought to study. A serious student would want to question, for example, why the purveyors of the potions and lotions all wear black smocks that make them look like dragon ladies under the fluorescent lights.

Another topic that should be studied is why women are so willing to fork over $50 for one product in a line of many and then feel good about that outlay. Especially when $2.50 would buy us a bar of soap that would do just as good a job of cleansing the crud off our faces.

And take a look at the packaging. You can choose bottles with little doves on top, things with gold or silver lids, dome shapes with soothing lime greens and silver lettering or the quietly-elegant bottle of amber liquid with maybe a crown of jewels on top, fake, of course.

As if the unique flasks weren't enough to titillate the senses, the bottles will be placed artistically in a tote bag that looks like a dreamscape, after being wrapped in a piece of gold tissue that you want to salvage and put on your coffee table.

The sales pitches are a study in themselves. The cosmetic saleswoman is so well trained she could probably keep up a steady stream of flattery for 15 minutes without taking a breath. But when you ask a hard question, like 'What can you do about the wrinkle that shows up in your neck about age 40?" all she can think of is, *Wear turtlenecks.* You don't dare ask her whether the products originated in a slaughterhouse or abortion clinic, like spoilsport news reporters and consumer advocates maintain.

I'm sure our sisters way back down the ages succumbed to traveling peddlers with little pots of dyes and potions of snake eggs to make them look younger and attract their favorite male. So, this is nothing new.

I guess it's fun to take a day out to be flattered and made to smell like a French whore. But I went home with a headache and watery eyes and found myself trying to recall the lines of a poem that glorify wearing purple and learning to spit on the sidewalk when you get old. That sounds like a heck of a lot more fun than trying to tame wrinkles. *March 17, 1993*

This interactive column restricted to bifocals

In trying unsuccessfully to keep up a pace that would be grueling for a 20 year old, it occurs to the Mad Mother that it's time for another old fogey column.

You know you're an old fogey when...

•You take a shower with a tree frog and don't even notice it until you put your glasses back on. Then you call your 11-year-old son to retrieve the slimy thing.

•You consider playing a hot game of cards a physical activity that burns calories (and no, I'm not referring to strip poker).

•You admit that maybe you're getting a little past your prime and instead of dreaming of someday buying a boat to pull you on water skis, you set your sights on a little two-person fiberglass jobbie that has space for Ma and Pa's fishing gear and a cooler and only needs a trolling motor instead of a 75-horse motor.

•You begin fixing your hair in a new style that hides the numerous strands of that different color at the temples.

•The highlight of your day is watching the sunset, and the best entertainment is afforded by a squirrel chattering on a utility line.

•You get a kick out of looking and laughing at the quaint

clothing and hairstyles in a 1980 yearbook and then recall you graduated almost a decade earlier than that.

•Whenever someone asks, you can't remember your own age.

•Someone gives you a cap that says "Old Fart" on it.

•You're too vain to get real bifocals and refuse to crane your neck to look through and adjust to lineless lenses, so you spend all your time peering over the tops of your specs.

•You'd really like to get a vein job done on your legs but don't think the pain will be worth it.

•You start searching out magazines and catalogs that feature older models and really appreciate the flyers that use un-model-like employees with paunches and receding hairlines.

•You think it's a rule to be in bed by 10:30.

•You begin to guess someone's age by looking at their knees.

•You get lost in mid-sentence.

•You get lost in mid-thought.

•You get lost on your way to the refrigerator. *September 27, 1995*

Older student seeks younger, fresher brain cells

A lifelong learner. Doesn't that have a nice ring to it?

At least I liked the sound of it when I enrolled this winter in an online journalism course, the first step in getting a master's degree. Don't know for sure what I'll do with one of those advanced degrees, but, by golly, it'll look good on a resume in case I ever fire myself as a publisher.

Little did I know that becoming a student in advanced middle age is not as easy as it looks in the course catalogs.

Nowadays, you have to know quite a bit about using advanced technology. Sure, I'm computer literate and can surf the net a little. I do click the mouse too fast and don't watch what's happening, then wonder where the stuff went when it disappears. Which makes it a little tricky with an online class.

For starters, you have to load software on your computer that lets you "enter the classroom" and have a discussion with your teacher and classmates. That software has to be downloaded, and you need a special "key" to unlock it. The key is a number that only your teacher has access to. She gives it to you with a long sheet of instructions.

In the middle of all this key and classroom business, we're trying to get two internet servers to operate on three different computers and discover, after an entire weekend of pulling out our hair and talking to "techies" on the phone, that our system software on one of those computers isn't new enough to allow that.

Aside from technology challenges, there's one big thing I hadn't considered in becoming a student again—homework. Of course, I could have chosen a little more exciting class to start this new-old experience. I picked Media Law.

Have you ever read 62 pages of legalese on a dreary Sunday afternoon? Trying to get interested in constitutional law and become passionate about the First Amendment and what the Founding Fathers really meant is not my idea of Sunday recreation.

Here's my routine: Open the textbook. Do a Mr. Bean routine, lining up all your pens and highlighters in a row. Settle into the recliner in front of the picture window where there's plenty of light. Read the first few paragraphs ... yawn ... rearrange pens ... squirm.

This is the precise moment I discover that the new lineless bifocals I bought for vanity's sake were not going to be helpful. After fiddling with the glasses, squishing them to my head, then reading over the tops of them, I got 19 pages read. Time for a nap!

I found every excuse in the world not to study. I even tried getting Lemonade Man to take me to a movie, but he was too busy trying to get computers to talk to each other.

Fixing Sunday dinner was suddenly more appealing than reading about John Peter Zenger and *Madison v. Marbury*. I knew there was a reason I avoided a law class in undergrad school.

Only by sheer force of will and by getting a floor lamp from the basement and training two light sources on the book did I get those 62 pages read. And this is only the first week.

In our first online class discussion, we were introducing

ourselves and I immediately told everyone that I'm ancient. That will be my excuse when I become a dropout at age 49.

But Lemonade Man waves the check stub under my nose, reminding me what we paid for tuition. I'm stuck. I'm looking at The Kid, who never brings homework home and does fine on report cards and wishing we could manage a brain transfusion. I need some younger cells, quick! *January 1998*

No longer able to run through airports

When Mad Mother and Lemonade Man took to the friendly skies of American (faulty tail sections and all) on February 4th, we'd both been strangers to air travel for about six or seven years. A lot has changed in that time.

The biggest change has been in the number of electronic gadgets in evidence. And it's not that the cell phones and laptop computers were all that necessary on a Saturday morning. Most of the users were showing off.

As we picked up our bags at the St. Petersburg, Florida airport, one guy was talking to his bookie. Earlier, at our layover in Dallas, a plump mother with a cell phone attached to her like a child on a retractable cord, was giving her family a play-by-play: They've just called us for boarding ... I'm now boarding the plane ... I'm now picking up my Bistro bag snack ... I'm now looking for seat 24C...

The guy across the aisle on our flight to Florida got out his laptop immediately and said it's what he does now instead of reading a book. Helps the flight time go faster and he doesn't so much mind that he's scrunched in a narrow seat for two hours (those seats do seem to have gotten narrower in six years).

Me? I waited to use my laptop until we got to our condo, then used it to help put out three pages of this week's newspaper from Florida, thus ruining one day that was supposed to have been spent in the sun. But what the heck? It was just as warm in Missouri as in Florida anyway.

On the return trip, we did invest in a low-tech device that has now become a necessity for air travel. Got us one of those carts with wheels to put carry-on luggage on. If you've never tried to run from gate 14 in Terminal A of the Dallas airport to gate 39 in terminal C in only 15 minutes, you haven't lived. We almost died, actually, on the trip down.

It may be a long time before we fly again, but you can bet the laptop will be riding on that new little cart next time, instead of hanging off the shoulders of someone who got too old to run through airports. *February 2000*

The pluses and minuses of growing down

Big Guy's cousin was famous in the family for her belief that after you reached a certain age, you started "growing down." I'm beginning to think she was right.

At a weekend gathering, the women in the group had a gabfest about numerous medical problems that come with aging. We spent entirely too much time lamenting the medical profession's heavy reliance on diagnoses of hormonal imbalances for every malady from fuzzy thinking to headaches. We spent too little time discussing the freedom that comes with advancing age.

For example, this summer I've declared a personal ban on panty hose and makeup (except lipstick). And for the first time ever, I really don't care if anyone sees my extra flab and varicose veins while wearing a swimsuit.

At the ripe age of 50-something, I know I'm fighting family genes, the stress of being a business owner, and having a desk job, in my attempts to become more fit and healthy. So, why not enjoy yourself at this age, take yourself out of the prom queen competition, and live life authentically?

The only rule of thumb is not to get near too many three-way mirrors. And, when you do something that could be characterized as fuzzy menopausal thinking (such as not being able to get the key out of the car, calling the service department, and hearing the entire garage laughing at you because you forgot to take the vehicle out of reverse) then you just say, "SO WHAT!" Tomorrow the joke will be on someone else, and the world will forget about your stupidity.

Meanwhile, it's time to savor every moment and undergo periodic attitude adjustments. Just had one this morning upon receiving a news release advertising an open house this Saturday for the Forty Acre Club. The event is in recognition of National Nude Week. That little item served as a reminder that I'm not quite as liberated as the above would lead you to believe, since I'm not even tempted to participate. But for those of you who are interested, make your way to Lonedell, Missouri with the entire family in what's advertised as "an afternoon of hometown charm." *June 2002*

The inherited traits of packrats (hang onto your bungees)

I'm starting to worry about Lemonade Man as we head into the age of decrepitude together. He's becoming more like his father every day.

I never knew the man, but his actions are legendary. There are still many signs of them in the family house in south Kansas City. The former machinist was pretty handy around the house, but he needed to write reminders to himself and others about what they should and shouldn't do. There are black scrawled admonitions to "wipe your feet" at the back door.

The wiring in the house is so convoluted (make that dangerous) that switches to the utility room might be located in the back bedroom. They were labeled too.

And, because he saved pieces and parts of things in the event that he might someday need them, those pieces and parts often became the fabric of some strange contraptions, which then had to be labeled for the next generation to figure out. A repair man who came to check out the 50-year-old heating system that's been rattling a lot lately chuckled and shook his head at how cobbled things were. "Are you sure my dad hasn't been here and worked on this?" he wondered. Maybe all depression-era dads were the same. Perhaps all older men have the ingenious idea of putting all the appliances on wheels so they can be cleaned behind.

Well, our house doesn't yet have wheeled appliances, but man, do we have the hooks!

Every time we go to a hardware store or Wally world, we have to spend at least 15 minutes looking at hooks. We have imitation brass hooks in every bathroom, on the solid oak armoire (one for each of our bathrobes, which end up on the chair anyway), two in every closet, and quite a few outside the back door.

Lemonade Man has inherited his father's handyman abilities so much that all our kitchen counters now boast fluorescent lights. My sewing machine now has its own floodlight.

I'm not complaining, mind you. And it would be okay if we stopped at hooks and lights. What worries me now is stopping on the interstate to pick up a bungee cord that someone lost. Or, getting out of the truck on a cloverleaf in the city to pick up a blanket that blew out of a moving van.

"My dad would have stopped for it," he admits sheepishly. "Besides, we can use it." Never mind that the hooks on the bungee cord were so bent they were unusable. That meant another trip to the hook aisle.

I'm so worried about this tendency and its inherent meaning for already-bulging work benches and toolboxes, that I'm thinking of making a pact with him. I'll stop saving gift boxes and shopping bags if he'll quit collecting junk along the road.

Or, we can just continue our packrat habits and let people shake their heads about us at our estate sale. *December 2002*

Two self-saboteurs discover the South Beach Diet

Dieting is a dirty word in our house.

We've tried the Atkins, The Zone, the Pritkin, low-fat, low-carb...

We've bought books and bought books and all we seem to do is chew the covers.

Yes, we've tried exercise too and just ended up selling various pieces of equipment in garage sales. An expensive treadmill is in the basement garage right now, serving as a great beach towel hanger.

Psychology and reverse psychology didn't even work. You

know the drill: All you need to do is push back from the table. Or, if you'd stop bending your elbow so much, you'd lose weight, fatso.

Not even plastering a photo on the fridge of myself at age 22 in a bikini did the trick.

Early in our marriage, Lemonade Man brought in the bad habit of eating a bowl of ice cream or some other sweet snack while relaxing in front of the TV at night. Now, it seems like an autonomic response: watch TV, eat. Don't watch TV, eat anyway.

And his favorite snacks are watermelon and grapes—not bad, unless you're a diabetic.

So, imagine the consternation of two yo-yos like us when yet another diet promises to make us learn to eat right for the rest of our lives. Sure, sure, we said with a smirk, knowing we qualify as certified self-saboteurs.

Enter the South Beach Diet, on the wings of an email. Developed by a cardiologist (aren't all diets developed or endorsed by someone with two letters behind their names?) this regimen promised to take off between 8 and 13 pounds in the first two weeks.

Well, guess what? It took ten off me in the first week and seven off Lemonade Man. But it made us realize we're sugar and starch junkies. As I tearfully brought half of a Death By Chocolate cake to work for colleagues to consume and stashed all the bread in the house in the freezer for fatter days, we are learning to eat lean meat, lots of vegetables, olive oil, balsamic vinegars, cheeses, and fat-free, sugar-free Jell-O. Instead of opening a package of prepared, frozen stuff full of hydrogenated oils and preservatives for a quick dinner, I'm getting elbow exercise chopping and sautéing. Amazingly, the food has been wonderful, tasty, wholesome, and satisfying. I just dirty every pan in the house and never have a clean cutting board available.

There are other disadvantages to this new regimen.

•I have to walk past the snack box at work and pretend I don't smell chocolate.

•We have to sneak almonds and beef jerky into a movie instead of splurging on popcorn.

•Going to the grocery store is something to do only after you've had a meal or snack.

•Celery and V-8 juice are our friends, but not necessarily together, or with vodka.

•Just as I was learning to relish the taste of an occasional cold Miller's Lite on a hot summer afternoon, I learn that the dextrose in beer is the worst possible enemy of anyone wanting to lose weight.

•I have to endure an employee's detailed narrative of how to make toffee bars.

By this time next week, the highlight of our day will be allowing ourselves to eat a piece of fruit or a slice of bread. Maybe in three years we'll graduate to mashed potatoes again. *2003*

Young chick brain in old duck body

Our minds are sometimes our own worst enemies. They evidently don't really age with our bodies.

The mind says, "You're still a young chick." The body replies, "If I'm still a young chick, why does it take me so long to get up off the floor? And why can't I ride my bike anymore?"

That's what the body said to me last week after Lemonade Man aired up the tires on our bicycles and I took mine out for a spin.

We have a quarter-mile long asphalt driveway that curves and bucks across our 15 acres. That driveway is the bane of our existence during winter ice and snow, since its lowest part forms a dam between a pond and a creek. Both sides of the dam have 15-foot drop-offs. When we moved to the country, I sort of suggested that we put up some kind of guard or CCA fence that would keep a careless driver (wonder who I could have been thinking of?) from sliding off into never-never land. The suggestion was met with a raised eyebrow of denial.

Back to the bike. You can't imagine how much fun the young chick brain thought it was to whiz down that steep, curving drive on two wheels, wind flying through my hair, bugs glancing off my teeth and glasses. Even having to shift gears and use some leg power on the uphill side wasn't so bad. It was upon arrival at the top of the hill, before the driveway crosses a cattle guard, that was the booger.

The old duck brain finally kicked in at that point, telling me it was best to turn around and not cross the guard or get on the loose gravel road. It seemed better to apply the brakes and hop off, turning the vehicle around manually. That proved a little difficult, since the momentum was on the downhill side and I wasn't totally upright.

I thought of Ruth Buzzi in the old *Laugh In* shows. Like her, I fell off my "tricycle," sideways, in slow motion, with the thing landing on top of me. I now have the battle scars to prove my adventure. But I have to say, warm asphalt felt nice for a few minutes, until I started laughing hysterically, then realized I would soon be sporting some blue and purple spots on various body parts.

The young chick brain tries to tell me things like I can stay up until midnight watching a movie and not pay for it the next day. It lies. It also tells me that putting 25 pitchforks full of grass clippings on a garden and bending over pulling weeds is a piece of cake. It is, for the first five minutes.

And these days, when I happen to look at my hands, they're the hands of a stranger who has seen more dishwashing than hand lotion, more garden dirt than manicures.

Maybe the brain is just trying to be merciful when it tells us we're younger than we think we are. I'll try to remember that when I'm ready to get on the bike again. *June 2003*

On being initiated into the society of those who have cameras stuck down their throats

Modern medicine is a marvel. Twenty-five years ago, who would have dreamed that a doctor could stick a flexible tube with a camera on it down your throat to check out the health of your innards?

I was the privileged recipient of that procedure Monday morning. It's called endoscopy, for those of you as yet uninitiated into this medical miracle. The only painful part of the whole thing was getting a pointy metal thing stuck in the back of my hand to feed in pain killer and anesthesia.

The worrisome part of such procedures is that the wrong person or persons will obtain access to that drug they give you to forget. It's the stuff of science fiction films—give someone a drug, then have their kids stolen by aliens for some awful experiment in a spaceship. The poor parents forget they ever had kids and try to build a new life but they're never happy. Does this sound like a Dave Barry column or what? But it is something we need to worry about, along with getting stuck in mammogram machines and having a plane crash into your house.

Back to reality. The last thing I remember before the foreign liquid began dripping into my veins was having what looked like a dental appliance shoved in my mouth. The brochure said I'd be conscious but relaxed and have short-term amnesia. (They didn't know I have that a lot without drugs). Did I somehow manage to tell a bad joke through that mouthpiece or otherwise embarrass myself? What did they really do to me? I'll never know. I can't even remember calling the office a few hours after the procedure to tell the girls I do have a hiatal hernia, a stomach polyp (which they removed through their magic little tube), and acute gastritis. All I know is I slept better yesterday afternoon than I have in years. And the best part? I got a souvenir photograph of my esophagus and its nasty little hernia. Now that's one for my family photo album! *April 2005*

The alien that now inhabits our bedroom

While we Americans are good at accusing insurance companies of practicing medicine by telling doctors and hospitals what they'll pay for and for how long, some of us become savvy enough to work the system to our advantage.

You quickly learn, once you meet your high deductible, to get all those long-delayed health things taken care of before the deductible rolls over again.

That's been the case with me this year. I met my deductible in January with a simple little sleep study at Cameron Regional. From my father's side, it seems I've inherited sleep apnea. That's where you stop breathing enough times a night, in between loud, honking snoring, to make your mate shake you awake for fear that you'll perish in your sleep.

My aunts and uncles rely on Ambien for their sleep apnea (which totally appalled a respiratory therapist who told me it would cause even shallower breathing). Not me. I am now the proud owner of a breathing machine, which goes by the name of CPAP.

This machine is a little tabletop number that forces air through a tube and into your nostrils during the night. It won't win any prizes for sex appeal. Matter of fact, when you put the harness over your head, strap the mask to your nose, and settle down for a decent night's sleep, you look like a creature from *Close Encounters of the Third Kind*. The first night I wore it, I sat up in bed to turn over and the dogs started barking at the strange creature they saw.

I'm getting used to having a chipmunk ring around my face from the impression left by the mask. It's become my status symbol, a sign of a modern ailment that undoubtedly has some of its origins in sitting for too long in front of a computer and eating too many processed foods on deadline days.

A fellow newspaper publisher who has had her machine for months told me she went to a state press convention in the fall and immediately recognized the tell-tale ring-around-the-nose of a colleague. They immediately began trading notes on their shared ailment. I'm sure a formal support group for CPAP users and apnea sufferers is already a reality.

Meanwhile, I'm enjoying sleeping solidly through the night, having more energy, and not snapping everybody's head off. My mate is also sleeping better and there's much less of sending me into the guest bedroom where my snoring doesn't bother him.

I'll happily be the poster child for the CPAP industry, but I'd like to stand in line for the next-generation equipment—something in pink, perhaps, and something a little sexier than having a tube running from your nose to a bedside machine. But then, I guess an alien outfit is a small price to pay for staying alive a little longer.
May 2005

Can we blame bumps on the head or use age as an excuse?

I can't count the number of times I've told people that this is a business to keep you humble. How can you ever have a big head about anything when you call people by the wrong names on the front page of the paper?

I'd like to offer the excuse that I cracked my head on the basement stairs while putting away Christmas decorations a few weeks ago. I truly haven't been the same since that date, but there's a little blank spot in my synapses that began opening up years ago, causing strange behavior, like referring to someone by their maiden name when they've been married for at least a decade. It'll also result in seeing someone on the street that I know almost as well as my own relatives and their name will not come forth from my addled brain to my lips.

Lemonade Man suffers from the same affliction. An employee who's been with us for months came in the office for a non-work-related errand and my mate looked at me blankly and said, "Now who was that?" I started to reply, "She's our employee, you idiot," but remembered that the day before he'd dropped the freezer lid on his head.

I'm sure we have more of the same blank spots to look forward to and can only hope that younger people in our lives will be sympathetic and patient with our failings. If not, we'll have the gleeful satisfaction of saying, "Wait until you get to be my age!"

I'm wondering if, along with the blank brain spots, we can anticipate becoming more cantankerous and set in our ways. I know at least one couple that is becoming more territorial, for example. We wonder why our animals growl and hiss when their space is invaded. I was doing some interior hissing while I watched Lemonade Man appropriate my favorite measuring cup for his plants. I wondered how long this cup that I use at least three times a week would sit on the kitchen counter with potting soil in it. Finally, this morning I asked if it would be possible to use my own measuring cup again or if I needed to buy a new one. He reluctantly agreed to relinquish it if I'd put the dirt in a bowl (again from the kitchen cabinet!). Then I recalled how miffed I was to think I'd lost a half cup measure for a year and finally rediscovered it in a container of dry dog food.

Turnabout came when I complained to Lemonade Man later about the fact that the broom and dustpan in the garage was never put back in the same place. "Whose garage is it?" was the reply. "Whose kitchen is it?" I countered. We were even, for now. *2005*

Learning to appreciate the gift of parsley flakes

You know you're aging when your bowels become an appealing topic of conversation.

For the past two years I've ignored my gynecologist's recommendation to have a baseline screening colonoscopy. Just the thought of having a photographic device intrude where no camera has ventured before left me shuddering in horror. But the ordering of another test to check out the progress of my hiatal hernia led to the economical decision to use anesthesia for two jobs instead of one. Besides, the American Gastroenterological Association recommends colorectal screening for people without any risk factors beginning at age 50. I am past 50.

Recognizing the need for something like this, and putting your best psychological feet forward, are two entirely different things. The dread began at bedtime last night. Just following the prep schedule—figuring out when to take a laxative, when to take the Fleets Phospho-soda—and the thought of forcing 32 ounces of fluids down the gullet between 7 p.m. and bedtime tonight kept me wide-eyed until midnight.

The toughest, of course, is not eating anything solid for 36 hours. For a veteran and champion consumer of food, it's the challenge of a lifetime.

As I've been drinking my meals today, I'm learning that a newspaper is a horrible place to work. Since we're under constant deadline stress, we think we are required to have a ready source of snack food. This morning, I had to slap my own hand as it was reaching for the chocolate-covered peanuts on the lunch table. It was just a Pavlovian response to dig in that little bag.

It's our longstanding tradition to have a snack break on deadline day, complete with high carbs and lots of sugar, with a little caffeine on the side. As I made three different flavors of Jell-O this morning to serve as my treat, what do I spy but a box of Casey's donuts.

The highlight of excitement in my day of gastronomical torture was discovering that the low-fat chicken boullion I poured in boiling water for lunch contained parsley flakes. I don't know if that was legal or not (can you see through a parsley flake?) but it could be the psychological boost I'll need to get through the rest of the day.

I don't have a lot of help from my partner, who probably needs a colonoscopy himself. He taunted me at lunch, crunching his fresh potato chips in my ear. After lunch he talked about going out by himself for a steak dinner while I again feast on boullion, then asked me if I wouldn't like a grilled bratwurst right now. I asked him how he'd like a poke in the eye with a sharp stick right now.

I have tried to trick myself into thinking I'm being treated like royalty on a liquid diet. Brought a fancy teapot to work, and a crystal bowl to hold the four different colors of sugared cow hooves that are the day's dessert. But, like the advice I once took to make bill paying a special occasion by accompanying it with a glass of wine and some good music, the mind is no fool. It knows when it is being deprived of donuts and chocolate-covered peanuts.

The only consolation to this is remembering that I have some chemically-sensitive friends who go to a clinic in Dallas for regular colon scrubbings. And they do this voluntarily! When faced with the imagined process of having a Brillo pad used on your innards, I'll count myself lucky to have a little fiber optic scope in there for a few minutes tomorrow.

And for all those who haven't yet faced this milestone in the aging process, I have only this to say—your turn will come. *2006*

On being shown the light of senior citizenship and all its wonderful benefits

"You wait until you get to be my age," Lemonade Man has warned me for the past five years. He's referring to the aches and pains and discomforts of senior citizenship. After the week just finished, I'm beginning to see the light of his wisdom.

Trouble is, I'm also beginning to get sick of myself as I conduct a daily inventory of the aches. Let's see—today, the elbow that I hyper-extended in moving extraneous junk to the shed has flared up, issuing a painful reminder that it's once again time to get out the Ibuprofen cream. Then there's the right hip that gave me fits all night, no matter which position I tried to get to sleep in. That annoying ache is making it difficult to navigate the stairs or walk more than three steps without wincing in pain. Could it be time for another cortisone shot, or maybe the more drastic joint replacement that is sure to be in the cards?

And we can't forget the little toe on the right foot that snagged on my slacks this morning, being bent plumb backwards, or the three toes on the left foot that I managed to ram into a clothes basket in the dark a few nights ago.

Other signs of physical decline in this decade are apparent in the fact that I can no longer stand at the stove for hours, then bend over to retrieve something in a bottom drawer and quickly straighten up again without a loud moan. And I would really appreciate lessons in the correct way to peel myself off the floor after rummaging around in the bottom of a cabinet for a stupid lid to put on leftovers. Does one haul the carcass up by pulling it along the countertop, or is it better to do a Yoga stance by curling up from the hands and knees into a crouch then pushing flat handed from the floor until you're bent in half like a clothespin, then reaching like a blind person for the countertop to use as a brace?

Big Guy got to watch such maneuvers recently and he wasn't sure whether to run to my assistance, call 911, or the nearest Weight Watchers chapter.

A few weeks ago, I told the hearing aid specialist we call on for advertising that Lemonade Man and I seem to be accusing each other of mumbling all the time now. It's difficult to count the number of times we ask for a repeat or mutter, "Say what?!" Even though we both attack the ear wax with Q-tips every morning, the world that we listen to is becoming less audible—to the point that upon asking my mate if his aching legs were feeling better after a hot bath, he asked me in exasperation, "Do I like peanut butter?! Why would you ask a thing like that?"

I could understand a similar miscommunication I had with his 73-year-old stepmother a few weeks ago. Upon telling the story of a man in their neighborhood who had hanged himself from a tree after episodes of running nude down the streets in the middle of the night, I inquired, "Do you suppose he was schizophrenic?" whereupon she replied, "Oh no, he wasn't friendly at all."

With all these side effects and symptoms, the only thing we seem to look forward to is traveling someday. But my sister-in-law, upon returning last week from a tour of the Holy Land, called with the strong imperative, "Get your traveling done now, before it's too late." Her bum knee acted up on the third day of the tour from all the stair climbing and walking she was doing.

But why should we worry about future impediments to our dreams of traveling the world? We're most concerned now with negotiating a family discount for hearing aids. *2007*

Getting hung up on shortcuts

Good help is hard to find.

After the man who has cut our three acres of grass for years decided to quit, Lemonade Man decided to take on our yard maintenance himself. It's such an onerous chore that this man, who needs hernia repair pretty badly, has decided to postpone surgery until winter out of fear I'll have to take on the mowing.

How quickly a yard can get away from the person too busy with other things. What really gets neglected is the weed whacking. You can put that little chore off for a couple of weeks. But when you have about a mile of board fence that you feel obligated to keep up like a Kentucky horse farm, it becomes pretty tedious. And even though I did my turn with a weenie, battery-operated weed cutter, it just wasn't good enough for the exacting master of our little estate.

"You've got to have enough power that it throws the grass all over your pants legs," he explained to me recently, comparing my toy to his bent shaft Stihl, with its God-only-knows-how-many rpms. I shrugged and decided to let him have all the fun Saturday morning while I stayed inside and worked on the computer. He was gone for well over an hour.

When he finally drug himself into the house, stripping off his jeans at the back door, he came in looking sheepish. "I got caught on the fence," he admitted.

"And?" I waited for the inevitable disaster story. In order to save time once he got to the end of the inside of the front fence, he decided to climb it. He carefully turned off the weed cutter and hoisted it over first, then began climbing the four-rung fence. Well, his leg was a little too short, or his back pocket got in the way. Long story short, he got hung up on the fence and couldn't get free. After injuring himself uncomfortably, he was interrupted by a passing motorist.

"Do you need help?" she called from her car.

"Yes," he admitted reluctantly.

"Where's your cell phone?" she wanted to know. "Back at the house," he replied.

"Oh, that's a good place for it. Sounds like my husband," she said. She had to dig in the knife just a little. Once she helped him get free from the pants-eating fence, she wanted to know what his next move would have been had she not happened to see his distress.

Without skipping a beat, he admitted that the next trick would have been to remove his jeans. She nodded knowingly and urged him to carry his cell phone at all times.

Now we're wondering if she was the one who drove by last year when Lemonade Man was using the weed cutter at the front fence and his pants just dropped suddenly to his ankles. She didn't help that time. Just about went off the road laughing.

If I had been in the same predicament, the fence, not the pants dropping, I would have ripped my pants to get unstuck and vowed never to climb a board fence again, even if it meant walking a few hundred feet to get to the other side. I'm just glad, for his sake, that the board fence wasn't barbed wire. *2008*

How much weight can an old wench winch?

Since Lemonade Man developed esophageal varices (enlarged blood veins in his throat) a few years ago, he's been restricted in his physical activity. If he lifts anything heavy or strains too much with his arms or shoulders, he could burst the varices and bleed to death quickly. To add to the restrictions, he needs shoulder surgery.

So, he has some pretty good excuses to get out of work these days. But he clings to his love of mowing with a zero-turn machine he calls The Bomb. He wasn't prepared to get his favorite toy stuck in the mud the other day.

He was hurrying to get some grass cut so we could go out of town to decorate graves and visit relatives the next morning. As he rounded my pathetic garden, the wheels on The Bomb began sliding. They soon sank axle-deep in the mud. He tried the rocking routine but only got stuck deeper. He tried calling the friend who helps us at the "farm," but he was unavailable.

He was then forced to admit his situation to me. That's never easy for a man who insists that mowing and using power equipment is solely the domain of males. He came huffing into the house where I was getting ready to throw some burgers on the female-friendly grill and said, "We've got a situation here. I got my tractor kind of stuck in the mud mowing around your garden." Notice the guilt-inducing use of the pronoun here?

I drop my meal preparations and head up to the garden, hands on hips, and disgust on my face. Yeah, he got it stuck bad and the dern thing weighs close to 1,000 pounds. I asked him if he had a come along. He sheepishly went to retrieve it and finally figured out how to pull out the straps. But the straps were too short to hang onto the tractor and any nearby support, so back he goes to the barn for a tractor chain. We hook it to the tractor where he says it should go, which is behind the machine and around a sapling. He thinks if we can winch it out, he can turn it around and go uphill and out of the mud. I think otherwise and try to tell him, but you know how stubborn men are. We did it his way—until it got stuck even deeper. Then we did it my way. *Can you sing it for me, Frank?*

We hooked the winch to the front axle of the mower and the tractor chain to a support post in the corral. I got on the business end of the winch and began cranking. Slowly that beast came out of the mud, as I was determined it would. If Lemonade Man had his way, it would have remained stuck until the mud dried up (it rained again that night).

The look on his face was now one of admiration and he almost asked to feel my arm muscles, but refrained, in case I got a swelled head. He just hadn't fully realized that this country woman had determination and fortitude enough to last until the next day when sore muscles set in.

On my way back to the house, I was already writing this column and the first thing that popped into my head was a tongue twister, "How much weight can an old wench winch if an old wench could winch weight?" How's that for warped? And while I don't really relish calling myself a wench, since the dictionary definitions are not all that nice, it's too alliterative not to use. *2011*

Part 8:

———

Laughing While Writing and Practicing Community Journalism

Backstory

I knew at a young age that I wanted to write for a living. I daydreamed of being a foreign correspondent and traveling all over the world. While waiting to achieve that dream, I served as the editor of my high school newspaper and the literary editor of the yearbook, whatever that title meant. Thanks to a trust fund set up when my father died in 1951, I was able to attend the University of Missouri School of Journalism, one of the country's most prestigious. The training I received there was intense and life-altering.

When my first husband and I returned from serving as Peace Corps volunteers from 1971 to 1974, we were determined to live near his parents, so we settled in the county seat of Kingston and ran a restaurant because there were no immediate openings for Mizzou-trained journalists in that rural area. Dan then got accepted to law school at Mizzou, so we left our home in Kingston for three years. I helped put my husband through law school by working for a state agency in Jefferson City, running press conferences and writing news releases.

When Dan got his Juris Doctor degree we moved back to Hamilton, where I began working as his legal secretary, all the while chomping at the bit to get back to writing. In 1981, I started work as managing editor of the Hamilton newspaper. In 1985, I purchased the paper, later acquiring the Braymer newspaper and combining the two.

For years I didn't pay myself a salary, operating the small-town paper as a "hobby" while gaining lots of satisfaction in the practice of community journalism. But when Dan and I divorced, paying myself and signing up for health insurance became a necessity.

Owning and operating a business through lots of tough economic times was always a challenge. Many times, I had no idea how I was going to pay employees or afford to make federal deposits for them for Social Security and Medicare. When Lemonade Man came into the picture, he became our CFO and engaged in lots of creative financing. But almost from the moment of joining me at the paper, he began a campaign to get me out of there and move to the city. I resisted for a long time, since I referred to the business as "my baby," while sacrificing time with my son for meeting weekly deadlines and reporting on school board and city council meetings.

As I told a friend just the other day, all I really wanted to do was write. At the newspaper, I had to be an advertising salesperson, an employee trainer and supervisor, and even a janitor. But I would not have traded the experience of writing weekly columns and doing feature stories for a different, higher-paying career. Our readers were like family to me. I loved being a big fish in a little pond and making that place a little better with the causes I supported or advocated. I relished the chance to make readers laugh, and operating a newspaper provided many opportunities for a little comic relief.

Go yipping gently into the night

In a survey of 1,000 amateur and professional golfers, 28 reported suffering from involuntary spasms, jerks, and tremors on the course. These jerks have a scientific name, focal dystonia, and the only cure is not to try so hard.

The focal dystonia had an unscientific name too: yip.

Doesn't that have a nice ring? You could impress your friends with that kind of term in your vocabulary.

Now when you're down to the last frame at the bowling alley and you need at least a spare to help your average and you blow it, you can just shrug your shoulders and say, "Well, I yipped that one."

Now, instead of arguing with your husband that you *did* keep your head down and your eye on that little, teeny golf ball, just tell him flippantly, "A yip made me do it."

It was a group of neurologists at the University of California-Los Angeles that conducted the above survey. We're not sure who invented the term "yip," but it must have come from Sesame Street.

There are those little outer space people that appear on the show with buggy eyes and dangling antennae. The critters go around checking out Earth's appliances (mainly radio and television) and all they ever say is a singsong, "Yip! Yip! Yip! Uh huh! Uh huh!"

I'd say they have us pegged pretty well.

At least two people in this world don't have the Mad Mother pegged very well. At a weekend gathering one woman approached me and asked me if I was the Mad Mother. I thought about lying but finally fessed up and she asked to take my picture. Maybe she needed it for evidence.

Another dear lady asked me the same question and said the only reason she took the paper was to read my writing. Imagine the burden of having someone say that to you! Now, when I have writer's block and the normally inane sounds closer to insane, I'll see that loyal reader's face and think how disappointed she'll be.

She also said that I must be a superwoman to be able to handle two businesses, a family, and community activities.

I should have invited her to my house and given her a guided tour of dust bunnies, shown her the four books I've started but not finished reading, the mending that's piled up all year, the bills that go unpaid because I don't have time to sit down and write checks. I could have tugged at her heartstrings by showing her a five-year-old boy who thinks his mother goes to meetings for a living and who invents just one more "secret" so he can delay Mom on her way to work so she'll spend a few more seconds with him.

There is no superwoman suit hanging in my closet. Jut a frayed work uniform that says, "Life without challenges and growth is not life." And there is also a bundle of sacrifices stuck away in the corner of the closet that hasn't even been examined.

And every once in a while, I wear a shirt that says, "Beware! Yipping woman. Approach at your own risk." *June 1989*

The sacrifices we make for good column material

It's always fun for column writers to get feedback from their readers. Evidently lots of you identified with taking shortcuts to do household chores and getting stuck on your roof.

Cecil Christian came in and offered me his extension ladder next time. Even volunteered to bring it over. I think he's worried about my longevity. After the column about the speeding ticket, he brought me in a little saying, "Anyone who drives like the devil may soon meet him." That slip of paper is now on the wall of my office, but maybe it should be on the steering wheel of my speed mobile.

After reading of my first fishing expedition, Johnnie Henderson loaned me a videotape, "Man's Favorite Sport," with Rock Hudson and Paula Prentiss. Wish I'd seen it before writing that column. It's a real gut-splitter. But even more revealing is the societal values you can pick up on when you watch an older movie. Didn't realize how much the sixties glamorized smoking and drinking. Every single woman in that movie smoked. Maybe the tobacco companies gave free cigarettes to all the movie sets in those days. Gosh, that was almost 30 years ago!

The last time Bob Hines came in, he said, "There's the woman who has more happen to her than anyone else in the world!" Now that's not entirely true.

Here's a little confession. There is a bit of hyperbole that goes into every humor column, but at least it's fiction based mostly on fact.

The following is not fiction.

Last night The Kid urged me to make the shutters on the house crooked and break a few windows, "just for Halloween, so it will look like a spooky, haunted house. Then you can fix it back."

Yes, column fans, this is the reason I nearly kill myself making house repairs—just so I can do something destructive and ugly to it to satisfy an eight-year-old's whims. Next time I'll make him play in the tar and climb the roof. *October 1992*

Now accepting nomination for Screw-Up of the Year

The Central Missouri Press Association has a traveling trophy that is the fear of everyone who has never received it. It's a wooden plaque in the shape of the state. Conspicuously mounted in the center, at an angle, is a large brass screw. The award is entitled, "Screw Up of the Year."

A colleague got it last year for an ad that appeared in his newspaper with the punchline to a raunchy joke. It had been written on the ad copy by the ad saleswoman, and the compositor didn't question it when setting the ad. Fortunately the punchline was indecipherable out of context and the advertiser who was its victim took it well. He even used it to his advantage in the next ad, inviting customers in to hear the rest of the story that went with the punchline.

If Northwest Missouri's press association had a similar award, it might have gone to a publisher north of here who wrote about a horseshoe pitching contest in a front-page article. When the story went through spell checker, the electronic gremlins turned the horseshoes into whorehouses.

Well, now the egg is on our face. We'd win the screw-up award hands down.

Last week's front page carried an article about three reported cases of AIDS and three of HIV in Caldwell County. It was important to me to make local folks aware that AIDS is not just a city epidemic. It's getting into the heterosexual population and is definitely something we should be aware of in rural Missouri. But somehow that message was diluted because right next to the large AIDS headline was a photo of two football players and their coach. The boys were presenting Coach Fairchild with a game ball for his 100th career victory. Now, with the newspaper folded, it looked like the AIDS story and the picture of the three next to it were related. In fact, one nine-year-old boy came home from school telling his mother emphatically that a boy the family knew had AIDS.

Never in our wildest dreams did it occur to us at pasteup that anyone would link those things. Once you unfold the paper, it becomes obvious they were two separate stories.

Coach Fairchild took it like a trooper. In fact, it was fodder for lots of good-natured joking. And we know now that people are reading the paper, just not carefully.

And speaking of carefully, we're instituting new pasteup procedures. There will be a large, dotted line across the middle of the page in special blue ink that will say, "This is the fold, dummy. Check it out!"

Doesn't it make you feel good when someone like me screws up so royally? It makes you sigh and smile and say, "Well, she took my screw-up quota for the week."

It's nice to be so useful to people. *November 1993*

The occupational hazards that beset column writers

Okay, gimme a break! The first time in ten years I haven't had a column and boy, do I hear about it!

"Letters from Home" last week fell victim to the occupational hazards of journalism. Two of the worst of these hazards are running dry and selling short. Sorta sounds like a poker hand or playing the commodities market, doesn't it? Well, journalism is like both of those.

We columnists do occasionally run dry on ideas. You sit staring at the computer screen an hour before deadline, hoping the diodes will give you inspiration. Sometimes they do, sometimes they don't. Last week they didn't.

Then we have the problem of general malaise that strikes column writers who go through spells of non-activity (the selling-short hazard), usually induced by the cruddy weather we've been having.

This past week, for instance, your mostly-faithful column writer hasn't done anything exciting, unless you count figuring out how to install the new pneumatic door opener I bought two years ago. Or finally learning to program the VCR so I can record a National Geographic special I won't be home for. Or cleaning out drawers and a closet.

This is mundane stuff and not worthy of a column.

The other occupational hazard we journalists are always prone to is "diarrhea of the computer." This can lead to glaring omissions and just plain stupid mistakes.

Like the Wisconsin newspaper contest I helped judge last Friday. The state has a screw-up of the year award and a room full of journalists had a real hard time deciding between the two entries. The first appeared at the end of an obituary and it read, "Leave this as-is because the jerk at the funeral home wants it as-is."

The other mistake appeared in a grocery ad. It was supposed to have read, "Ore-Ida Crinkle Cut Potatoes." The word "cut" had an extra letter in it that occurs somewhere near the middle of the alphabet.

When you get down to it, what we as writers do isn't nearly so amusing or interesting as what our employees or readers and their grandchildren do and say. Employee Kathy McIntosh's granddaughter had another jewel this week. She was excited about a little friend who was going to get a puppy. After excitedly detailing this important event, she told her grandparents she thought the breed of dog was a "bulldozer" and added thoughtfully, "Those bulldozers get mean, don't they?"

Column readers are like mean bulldozers when they don't get their weekly quota of inanity from this space. So, I'll try to do better and not miss any more columns. Okay? Now get off my case! *April 1994*

Warning label: Suitable only for the eyes of old geezers and baby boomers

Columnists just love it when they can add their two cents to lists of things. We think we're so clever and original when we're just putting something in words that everyone else has already thought of and just never written down.

With that in mind, it's time for me to make two additions to lists of things—the first to a list of small-town unique features.

You know you're from a small town when you recognize someone's dog away from home before you recognize its owner. The dog in question was Patches, owned by Clifford Scott. On our way to St. Joseph Sunday to deliver our *Rural Living* publication to stands there, we overtook a motorcycle bearing a short, white dog.

We were marveling at how a dog could balance on the back seat of a cycle without a restraint of any kind and were staring at the feat all the way past the scene. Suddenly, recognition dawned, but it was the dog we recognized first. Evidently, when Clifford fires up the motorcycle, it doesn't move without Patches on the back. Amazing! But I wonder if they make doggie helmets?

The other list to add to is one of those "You Know You're Getting Older" things.

I knew I was getting older this week when I read a portion of a Dave Barry (world's funniest writer) column to my journalism class and instead of laughing hysterically like I had, they looked at me like I'd lost my mind. I had thought it so appropriate to introduce my lesson on grammar and usage. Barry was posing as Mr. Language Person and answering questions about spelling.

Maybe the reason the younger generation doesn't appreciate Dave Barry is because he's now past 40 and enjoys writing about the illogical humor in things like the difference between criteria and criterion. My class had evidently never heard the words before. They weren't about to bust their guts over his definition of criteria as what presidents have to have to get elected (hair) and of criterion as a kind of car. Come to think of it, they've evidently never heard the word "subtle" or the phrase "play on words." Maybe they'll get old someday and develop an entirely new and warped sense of humor.

And a sense of humor may be what all of us need to get through the rest of the week. As this is written, ice is encrusting everything that doesn't move. Reminds me of the great ice storm of nineteen eighty-something when the power was off for 18 hours. We were forced to trot down the street to Grandma's and use her gas stove to eat and her old-fashioned heating stove to keep warm by.

What will I do now? Grandma's gone and my gas stove is fired by an electronic ignition. I do have a fireplace and maybe could figure out how to cook something in it. How does a fireplace-warmed Pop-Tart sound? Dave Barry would take that and run with it, but only us old geezers would find humor in it. *December 1994*

When it rains it pours, then you step in doo-doo

I should've gone back to bed this morning and canceled the day.

Even though the sun was shining for the first time in what seems a millennium, something kept closing my eyelids and whispering, "Don't do it! Don't get out of bed! The day will be just fine without you!" But one of three weekly deadlines beckoned, so I tempted fate and crawled out to face reality.

It was capital R reality that smacked me in the face when I entered the garage to leave for work. What in the world was the black streak on my bumper? Above the paint-peeled bumper was a crumpled light housing and above that, a buckled hood. Could someone have entered my locked garage in the night?

Then I recalled a late night at the city council meeting and a parking lot full of cars and trucks, leaving me no space to park except at the end of the lot, but still allowing plenty of room for a pickup parked by the dumpster to exit. Evidently it wasn't enough room.

Parked vehicles are sitting ducks in this town. Just over the weekend, the newspaper van parked behind the office was the victim of someone angry enough to hit the side mirror with a fist and break the glass. We know it was a fist because part of the skin from the fist is still on the mirror. Just like part of a white truck bumper is still on my front bumper.

Yes, it was a lovely day in the neighborhood. It got lovelier when, on the way back from getting a repair estimate, I stepped in something that should have been in a hog lot. Or, it could have been a dog pen. I didn't do a complete sniff test.

As my insurance agent said, it could have been worse. He's right to put things in perspective like that. I could have been in the parked car when it got hit. I could have been on the highway in the car. I could have been test-driving a brand-new car and had an accident. I could have lost my whole shoe in a real hog lot. I could have fallen entirely into a hog lot. I could have gotten lost on my way to work. Thank God those things didn't happen or that would really make it a bad day.

In the meantime, I'm trying to kick in the comprehensive

coverage on the car by convincing the agent that Monday night's city council meeting qualified as a riot or civil commotion. *May 1995*

Meat cleavers and missing brooms

Somebody needs to do a study on the ulcer and heart attack incidence among newspaper editors and publishers. They say dentists are the most stressed group of professionals, since they have such tight spaces to work in. But after a few mysterious events of the past week, I'm not sure our own profession doesn't have them beat all to heck.

Besides the perpetual worries about whether or not our postage bill will go up again twice in the same month (it did in March), and whether we'll make the weekly deadline without having to work until 2:30 a.m. before a press deadline of 8:00 a.m. (we did last week), you get to worry about how the readers will react to the words you write.

Some of them, knowing the publisher makes a habit of not getting to work until 8:30 or 9:00, come in the office and plant seeds of fear. Like the white-haired gentleman who popped in at 8:00 last week and told the receptionist, "Tell Anne I came in with a meat cleaver."

He never showed up and all I can think is "Good Lord, what did I do wrong this week?"

And then there was the case of the kitchen broom. We found a note on our display for rubber stamps. The cryptic message said, "Your kitchen broom has been kidnapped. If you ever expect to see it alive again, go to the Gould Farm Bridge on Saturday night and you might find it hanging." Ransom was 1,000 pennies in a dirty sock.

Is someone trying to make me lose my sanity—what little I have left? They're doing a pretty good job. *1996*

A woman's worst nightmare: Where are all the safety pins?

What's your worst nightmare? Missing the bus and having to

walk to school? Finding yourself in the buff in the middle of a crowd? Being late for a final exam?

How about breaking the zipper on your pants in the middle of a newspaper convention?

I worried about the problematic nylon zipper on my favorite winter pantsuit as I put it on last Friday and headed out the door for the 130th annual meeting of the Northwest Missouri Press Association. The back-closing zipper had given problems before, but only at the end of the day and in the safety of my own bedroom. It wasn't until after lunch Friday, before the afternoon session started, that it seemed past time for a pit stop. There, in the stall of the Ramada Inn restroom, a heart attack almost occurred. The zipper had separated with the pull tab at the top.

"Okay," I told myself, taking a few calming breaths and exhaling through my mouth (a throwback to Lamaze classes 19 years ago), "I can get this figured out!"

Somehow, I managed to scrunch the pants over hips to get a closer look at the offending aperture. But in trying to get the zipper to move, the metal tab at the top broke off, leaving no way to maneuver it up or down or sideways.

After a few minutes more of panic and deep breathing, the zipper did come all the way down. So, get back in pants, zip up, and go back to meeting. But wait a minute! What was that breezy feeling?

The zipper had separated again. There was no salvaging this pair of slacks. So, here I was, my pants stuck on me and some color-contrasting underwear hanging there for all to see. My coat was hanging on the back of my chair in the middle of the meeting room.

Should I scream for help and hope someone at the front desk hears? Should I streak through the halls, grab my coat, and never again face any of my colleagues (no doubt causing the writing of yet another convention legend, second only to the old publisher who got drunk and fell out of an upper story window of the old Hotel Robidoux).

I opted instead to call my husband on the cell phone in my

purse—a purse devoid of safety pins and other emergency supplies.

"You're what?!" he said in disbelief, not trying nearly hard enough to contain his laughter. "Do you want me to drive a half an hour to bring you some more clothes? Why don't you back into the room, grab your coat, and fly out of there?"

When I didn't buy that proposal, explaining that it was a back closing zipper to begin with, he suggested putting my pants on backwards and hiding the gaping hole with the front of my blouse.

Admittedly, the pants were stretchy. No one ever guessed that I sat through the rest of the meeting with backwards pants. I was the only one who knew that the pockets were going the wrong direction. *January 2003*

Another in a long line of life's little uh-ohs

It was another of those "uh-oh" moments last Tuesday—almost as bad as breaking a zipper at a press convention. This time it occurred as we were inching toward a deadline in a week with no news. The repeated and regular snowstorms had tended to make criminals and other newsmakers stay bundled up inside. I had left a hole on the front page for a photo of the only newsmakers in town last week—Secretary of State Matt Blunt and State Librarian Sara Parker.

Lemonade Man had left me with his truck, knowing that I'd need it later that night to inch down our steep driveway in four-wheel drive. About 2:45, before a 3:00 p.m. photo op, I decided I'd better start the truck and defrost it. It had only been sleeting for a few hours.

I'm a woman who admires and appreciates the technology that allows us to put a whole publication together, minus a hole on the front page, go take a photo with a digital camera, scoot back to work and, in a few seconds, fill the hole and put the paper to bed. But don't give me too many electronic gadgets, or I'll get confused.

That's what happened when Lemonade Man handed me the auto-start for his truck. Sure, he probably told me how to use it, but I'd never done it. I imitated his actions by standing inside, in the warmth of the office, pointing the gadget at the truck and pressing a button. Nothing happened.

In two seconds, I was outside, starting the vehicle like most sane people do, from the inside of the vehicle, with the key in the ignition. That's when bad luck took over.

It was obvious that the defrost mode would not thaw a quarter-inch sheet of ice from the windshield. Time to attack it with a sharp plastic instrument. But wait! What was that ominous sound?

The minute the door was shut, the automatic locks activated. The engine was running but I couldn't get inside to use it. The extra keys were 15 miles away.

Before total panic set in, a local helper arrived with three unique, low-tech tools—a rubber wedge that went in the top of the window, then something that looked like a blood pressure cuff which went in the side of the window, and a common coat hanger. I'm sure all good crooks have access to the same things.

In minutes the door was unlocked, and I was on the way, only 15 minutes late. The interim was filled with much wailing and gnashing of teeth, punctuated with an increase in the ferocity of the sleet raining down on my head.

Thus, we see that low-tech instruments have their place in a high-tech world. Thank God for them, and for their role in relieving another of life's uh-ohs. Now, if there was only a low-tech answer to the two-hour power outage we just went through, we'd sure like to know about it. If there was such a thing, I could have avoided writing this column twice. *March 2003*

True confessions about some less-than-ideal employees

Only someone dumb enough to write about a broken pants zipper would admit to the world that she has employed some criminals over the course of a 25-year career.

I was shocked Thursday night to see the face of a former short-term employee splashed all over the ten o'clock news. But there she was, Cassie M., convicted of defrauding the 9/11 victim's relief fund of more than $60,000 and facing 21 months in jail.

This is the same woman who did a brief stint of freelance

writing for us, claiming she had a journalism degree from Mizzou. She had the talent. And yours truly, ever the trusting soul, decided to hire her full-time about five or six years ago. She had a sob story that wouldn't quit about living in a car in Florida, being assaulted and left for dead, then coming back to her roots in Chillicothe. But I should have known that anyone who refers to her clothing as an "ensemble," with the French pronunciation to match, was a little suspect.

She penned a few columns on a freelance basis, detailing her writing jaunt in Kosovo, then did a well-researched and interesting series on landfills. But things began to unravel when she didn't follow my proofreading marks to correct a story. In response, she spouted off about Dean Smith of the journalism school. Knowing that was not the name of the dean, I placed a long-overdue call to my alma mater, only to discover that Cassie had not graduated from that institution. However, she had worked at the school's library. A call to that office resulted in the news that "Crazy Cassie" had indeed graced their walls and had gone by another last name in those days.

We immediately parted company with our little con artist, but not before helping her get a vehicle on installment payments from a Ray County used car dealer. The trip to look at that car was a memorable one for Lemonade Man. As they test-drove the car, she got ready to turn around and head back to the dealership when a portion of her anatomy became entangled in the steering wheel. They almost had a wreck, and now that corner of Highway 13 has been memorialized as Cassie's Corner.

Of course, she absconded with the car and never made another payment. And now we find out this creative woman went to great lengths to manufacture an identity for a non-existent brother who had supposedly been applying for a job at the World Trade Center on the day of the terrorist attacks. You've got to admire her imagination, even while you abhor what she did. She could have accomplished so much but chose to direct her energies to conniving and treachery.

Another former employee was cut out of the same cloth. She

was with us about as long as Cassie and attempted to sell ads. She talked a good line too. But it didn't get her out of prison a year or so later for the second-degree murder of an elderly lady in her care. From that employee I learned never to hire someone with violet contact lenses, especially when they tell you it's the real color of their eyes. *October 2003*

The self-appointed connoisseur of meeting room chairs

No one ever told us in journalism school that if we stayed in this career long enough, we'd become professional meeting attenders.

That probably only applies to small town newspaper writers, who have to sit through endless school board and city council meetings just to get some news in a place where murders and corruption do not exactly abound.

My predecessor in this newspaper used to greet the trains that came through Hamilton regularly in order to get the latest news. And those of us around here old enough to remember Leona Ralston can recall that she got a lot of news by just taking a walk. She even called her musings "Out Walking."

Things are different these days. There are no trains to greet and people generally hole up in their houses watching movies and World Wrestling Federation, so they're not out making news.

And so, we newspaper types go to meetings and high school sports events. In fact, I could probably go to a meeting every night of the week somewhere in this county. I balk at more than one a week, no matter how newsworthy the event. When you combine that with late night deadlines, my son and our dogs rarely get to see my face. But I'm not complaining, mind you.

I will, however, lodge my complaint about the condition of the seats at these meetings.

Take the city council meetings in Hamilton. While the aldermen and mayor sit on comfortably-padded chairs with arms, we peons in the peanut gallery sit on slightly-padded, narrow, metal restaurant chairs. While they stack neatly after meetings, after two-and-a-half hours of sitting in them, a condition develops that we refer to as TB. The first letter stands for tired. One of my fellow city council peons congratulates me each first Monday of the month if I don't snore through a portion of the meeting. I have to keep reminding myself that inquiring minds want to know about things like siphon pumps and repeater radios, or at least how much of their tax dollars go to buy such things.

Now the Hamilton School Board has much more comfortable chairs, nicely padded, and located just a few steps away from a drinking fountain. Occasionally these folks even share their break refreshments with me as a reward for sitting through MAP test results.

I have to award the Worst of the Worst Chairs Award to the county commission for the ridiculous excuses for furniture that occupy the circuit courtroom. These hard wooden things belong in a museum, they're that old. They have little rivets that will ruin a pair of pantyhose or snag your clothing. And they are guaranteed to cripple you if you have to remain in them for any length of time.

The only time I ever covered a three-day trial in that room, I took a pillow to sit on. This is not a place that a hemorrhoid sufferer can endure. This serves as my suggestion box message: Before the commissioners replace the walk leading up to the front door, they need new courtroom chairs. I know, as I'm the new self-appointed county chair chairman. *November 2003*

Help wanted ad plus confessions of a non-nimble-footed nitwit

Help Wanted: Need mature individual who is young at heart and nimble of mind and foot. Individual will be versatile and capable of multi-tasking, specifically able to train three new employees, take an ad order on the phone, and type a story, all at the same time. Maturity is needed for the position, especially when the file you've worked on for the past week, taken home to work on at night, and tried to finish on a deadline day, bombs and you lose it entirely.

Applicant will need to be schooled in biting his or her tongue and refraining from colorful language.

Further, the applicant will need more patience than the previous job holder when a computer crashes and loses all the Braymer news files on that same deadline day.

Nimbleness of foot is a must. Previous job holder never watches feet and when co-worker (husband of job holder) is attempting to set up a new computer, with wires and surge protectors taped temporarily to floor, found that kicking said wires and appliances can cause another computer to crash before it's even installed.

Individual who applies for this job must be willing to work long hours for little pay, and have a very tough hide, impervious to complaints about mistakes that appear in a very public space, once a week, for all the local world to see and snicker about.

The applicant will also possess a love of people and rural life and realize the comfort of knowing a lot of folks who make it all worthwhile by stopping by with a friendly smile, a joke, or a tidbit of news. Applicant will enjoy telling their stories, advancing their favorite causes, and celebrating their milestones.

Applicant will further realize he or she is an important cog in the big spoke of a community, helping grease that wheel with publicity and prods to the collective conscience.

This is an ad for my job—or should I say, my vocation. When I first began this column today, after the trials and tribulations of tasks that get ever more complicated and frustrating, I was halfway serious about replacing myself.

But upon further contemplation, the pluses usually outweigh the minuses. Tomorrow we will laugh about today's mishaps as the newspaper once again rolls off the presses. *May 2004*

Flicked switches that lead to lost columns and falling down jeans

I just finished writing one of the most beautiful columns of my career. In poetic prose I evoked the bittersweet feelings we all must have at this changing of the seasons. It had geese flying south. It had a farewell to the fishing pond, complete with me reeling in a four-pound largemouth, honest! It had a gardening goodbye in it. It even appealed to all the senses in a salute to fall, with references to hayrides, apple cider, and a side of beef fattening in a nearby feedlot, soon to be enjoyed as a Sunday pot roast.

You'd have loved it. I did, until it was extinguished when an employee's elbow knocked up against the light switch and shut off my computer.

And now, for the column I should have written in the first place. Forget the bittersweet. I'll bring on what you've come to expect from this space—another in a myriad of screw-up weeks.

It began for Lemonade Man with an agonizing Sunday of passing another kidney stone, after apparently knocking it out of its normal resting place by cutting cornstalks with a machete.

It continued its downhill slide with my annual trip to the gynecologist Monday afternoon (year-end rear-end, as a witty employee terms it). We like to combine trips, to make them count, so this one included a side trip to Mission, Kansas to pick up two used Macintosh computers to replace two older ones that got fried in the last lightning storm. After drooling over the latest bells and whistles on newer models, we loaded up our used purchases and headed home.

The next day, Lemonade Man prepares to install software and put the new used computers into service. After hours of fighting to get the acquisitions on the network, it becomes apparent that neither computer works. An angry Cherokee loads the heavy suckers into the back seat and makes another drive to Kansas with the offending hardware, ready to chew someone out royally.

Then this morning, above Cherokee decides to stop at the local carwash before arriving at the office. In the process of giving his treasured truck a bath, hose at carwash splits and sprays Indian into the middle of next week, giving him the second bath of the day. As he's fighting this new development, jeans that have been known to be problematic in the past fall to knees. With one hand on his jeans and the other still fighting the car wash hose, Man Who Is Beside

Himself forgets about washing truck and comes into office carrying office supplies (yesterday's trip also did double-duty) in one hand, holding up pants with the other hand and gritting the check ledger in his mouth. To all outward appearances, he'd had an accident that could have again been connected to kidneys.

Instead of going to Dollar General for a second pair of pants, he wrapped himself in a blanket and we put his jeans on the banister outside to dry. After all of us had laughed so hard we nearly had to change our own clothing, we reminded him of the suspenders that a subscriber brought in the office recently to help him avoid such incidents. We noted that they only work when attached to the pants.

In our more serious moments, we wonder why a black cloud follows our every attempt at maintaining at least a small degree of sanity in an increasingly-complex world. We realize that with the flick of a switch, we might lose everything.

Then I recall the poor individual I saw by the highway this morning, with all his possessions gathered around him, a scarf tied around his head to keep off the morning chill, and holding a sign seeking a ride somewhere east.

Just when the world seems bleakest and troubles mount, we can be thankful for our warm beds, for food on the table, for the beauty of the changing seasons, and for the ability we have to laugh at our own foibles. I might even find it possible to laugh at bumped light switches ... someday soon. *September 2004*

If he leads me to a microphone again, I will not follow

My youngest dreams of stardom in the music world were dashed to pieces at age five. It was on a family vacation. For some reason, the driver and passenger in the front seat did not appreciate my rendition of "The Star-Spangled Banner," sung non-stop at the top of my lungs for 45 miles.

Despite their screams to shut up, I got back at them years later with my brother on another vacation, both of us singing "100 Bottles of Beer on the Wall." I guess they thought that was the lesser of the other evils like, "Mom, make him stop looking at me!" or "She's got her hand on my side of the car!"

As a middle schooler, my only other foray into the world of potential singing stardom was at Longview Methodist Church when I sang a solo in front of the whole congregation. It was something like "For the Beauty of the Earth." I have no recollection of stage fright at that juncture in life. If it was present, it came back to haunt me as an adult trying to play the organ at church. I'd get so nervous I'd almost pass out. Neither fervent prayers for help from on high nor deep breathing seemed to help. I thought all that agony was in the past. But then came last Sunday.

The Kidder Christian Church attendance ranks were decimated by Scout camp, Guard duty, and the aftermath of The Kidder Picnic, with its Saturday night dance. So, when we showed up to do our weekly assignment for the Ecumenist column, there were only nine souls filling the pews of this 111-year-old institution. Minister Dorothy Knott greeted us warmly and immediately asked if we could sing. Lemonade Man quickly said he couldn't, and I said I usually try. That was enough for Pastor Knott. She announced she'd have some special music for us today. Little did I know the special music was me singing.

There I was, innocently taking notes about the order of the service when a song leader began leading several familiar old hymns. The pianist sang a solo and then sat back down in the pew. I was ready for the sermon, but that's when the bombshell struck. Pastor Knott asked me to come up front and lead the group in a favorite hymn.

First, I was speechless, then I declined, saying I wasn't prepared. Then Lemonade Man poked me in the ribs and said I had a beautiful voice. He got a dirty look from me with a promise to deal with him later. Thumbing through the hymnal, I found the shortest song possible, "Where He Leads Me," and went to the lectern, where I was handed a microphone that wasn't on. After whispering the first few bars (until I found the "on" switch), the words started to flow. My legs were shaking so bad I thought I'd collapse, but after a few "amens" from Pastor Knott at appropriate times, we got through the thing. Hopefully no one noticed that we didn't sing the refrain—ever. (It was in small print, under the verses, so I can plead nervous blindness.)

This column is to let my future church site pastors and song leaders have ample notice that church karaoke is not my strong suit, unless they enjoy watching nervous, knocking knees. I'm positive that, with my Grandma Garrett's girth that I've inherited in my 50s, it's not a pretty sight from behind.

My choice of hymns was appropriate, but I promise, I will not subject anyone to a repeat performance. I will not follow. Got it? *August 2005*

Fast Forward

Funny thing—I would eventually subject people to many repeat performances. Pastor Knott did not know she was laying the groundwork for me to become a future singer, and even a pastor.

When I sold the newspaper, I felt compelled to keep writing and trying to be funny. That spawned a retirement blog and the first iteration of this book, which led to helping other people publish their books.

When Marshall died in 2015, a portion of his life insurance went to starting a line of memoir products, and I continued to try to write funny blogs about retirement and widowhood. A few years later, I fell in love again, remarried, and moved back to my original hometown. My third husband, Wayne, graciously gave me the financial security and freedom to continue writing and growing in service to readers and new causes.

I rediscovered my singing voice by joining the Topeka chapter of Sweet Adelines International. With my new singing friends, I soon found myself writing and formatting a weekly newsletter and writing show scripts.

Wayne and I attended Sunday services together at the little church where I had gone to vacation Bible school as a child. That somehow led to the calling to become an authorized lay pastor for the Northwest Kansas Presbytery of the Presbyterian Church USA.

I'm now writing sermons and occasionally planning worship services.

I guess I can blame this on Pastor Dorothy Knott for leading me to the microphone that day.

And I guess I can blame (thank) the readers of *The Caldwell County News* for favoring me with their laughter and subscriptions and for giving me a sense of purpose and belonging for 27 years. I love coming back to Hamilton these days, running into old friends, and reliving memories of the life and laughter we once shared.

Other Books by
Anne Spry

Taking the Long Way Home: A Peace Corps Memoir of Brazil

Riding Rainbows Through the Storms: Finding Perspective and Hope by Journaling Through a Pandemic

Finally Noticing: Poems and Photos Prompted by a Pandemic

Journaling with Jesus: Writing to Heal from Trauma–A Masterclass by Cheri Battrick and Anne Spry

Searching for Summer: A Solved but Unresolved Missing Persons Case (co-authored with Brandy Shipp Rogge)

Rebuilding Your Life After the Death of Your Spouse: Experiences and Tips from Two Survivors by Anne Tezon & Craig Battrick

Tripping Down Main Street: The Fun and Funny of Community Journalism

Letters from Home: A Newspaper Column and a Memoir

About the
Author

After living in South America as a young woman, Anne Spry spent a lifetime seeking a stable home, mostly in Missouri. She put her journalism degree from the University of Missouri to work in a 27-year career as a newspaper editor and publisher in Hamilton. During that time, she also earned a master's degree in communication arts from Memphis State University. Instead of landing her a job as an instructor at her alma mater, like she hoped it would, the degree pushed her into working on book publishing even while running her newspaper. Once she sold the paper and moved to Kansas City, book publishing became her retirement avocation.

Destined for another move when her second husband died, Spry was blessed to go back to her roots and settle on ancestral land a few miles from where her parents grew up. She lives on five acres with incredible views of spacious Kansas skies, plants flowers, sings with a Sweet Adelines chorus in Topeka and is active in Kansas Authors Club.

Anne is married to Wayne, a retired military pilot. They enjoy spending time with Wayne's three children, grandchildren and great-grandchildren and sharing good times with Anne's three young grandchildren.

www.personalchapterspublishing.com

www.ingramcontent.com/pod-product-compliance
Lightning Source LLC
Chambersburg PA
CBHW021235130626
46554CB00004B/1503